To Peter and Lesley, May you enjoy Day Sixty Two in partic... [handwritten inscription]

[handwritten] 1/11/2008

THAT HEA

and the next 172 days

Dennis Berry

Published by Number 11 Publishing

THAT HEART ATTACK
and the next 112 days

ISBN 978-0-9555134-4-2

Cover design and artwork, The Design Shop
www.thedesignshop.co.uk

Printed in England by Printondemand-worldwide.com
9 Culley Court, Bakewell Road, Orton Southgate,
Peterborough, PE2 6WA

Number 11 Publishing
PO Box 459
New Malden
Surrey KT3 9DH

Printed in Great Britain for Number 11 Publishing

THAT HEART ATTACK
and the next 112 days

ACKNOWLEDGEMENTS

Dennis started writing this diary when he realised he had survived a major heart attack. Once he moved out of Intensive Care and found he could take an interest in the activities and people round about, writing it down became an incentive to get through another day. When he was back home and using his computer, this therapy helped him through the next stage.

Dennis had That heart attack just days before his retirement party from Kingston School of Architecture. This ultimately took place on 20th October and provided the conclusion to the present diary. He was overwhelmed at the number of people who sent goodwill messages, contributed to his retirement presents and came to the party; he says at one point in the book: *'There is no way I can think of to thank everyone other than perhaps through this diary even though no one will ever see it!'*

Thanks are due specifically to the following people: Dr Leonard Sherski, without whose prompt actions this diary could not have been written. His professional care, consultations on cricket and motor racing, and his friendship were much appreciated to the end. Michael Blackstock and Peter Jacob ensured that one of them visited Dennis every day and kept him just sufficiently up to date, while at home Carole and Graham Curson stimulated him with political argument and humour. You all encouraged his sometimes perverse perspectives on the stupidities of life - and Graham Bennett helped with this. Sue-Ann Lee and Carole Heatly have contributed their own well-chosen words for the back cover. To everyone who rallied round so magnificently – thank you so much. And to Jonathan, who said that reading the typescript earlier this year gave him yet another great conversation with his father – Dennis was very proud of you, too!

DENNIS BERRY
The same day, the year before

DAY ONE

It started like most days. Me, still abed, fuggy and night stale - she, fragrant fresh, bending over. "I'm off." The ritualistic one, one two three, kisses. The standard but so carefully phrased exchanges - "Take care... 'Bye for now... See you later... I love you... I love you..." Never goodbye. We are very careful.

The front door slams. The tap, tap tap, tap of her key on the wall above my head and she's off to catch the 7.27.

I get up slowly, stiffly. That lovely cup of reviver and then the paper. There is no rush, I do not intend to appear at college much before lunch today. I turn to my drawing board with pleasant anticipation, still in my pyjamas. The barn conversion, mark 2, is coming together very happily.

It must have been nearly eleven o'clock when the phone rang. Sandra wanted to know if the estate agents had sent anything.

Having got me off the drawing board and aware of the time, a bath seemed appropriate. Then, as ever, my regular exercise routine. A very gentle series of arm/shoulder and leg movements. The first of these to keep one-time frozen shoulders free and the second for dodgy discs. I have been doing these exercises for the last ten years or so and if they have not done much for my joints I guess they have been good for my ego. It gives one a sense of self-righteousness to say to one's unhealthy colleagues "Oh my word yes, I exercise for fifteen minutes every morning, don't you?"

It was while standing before the mirror that it started. A dull pain like indigestion in between my shoulder blades. It got worse. I fed my tie under my collar and felt the pain going down my arms. It filled my chest. I knew what it was.

"Please God, give me time."

1

I must not do my collar up, I thought and put my tie away into my pocket. The pain was heavy, crushing, bending me over it seemed.

"If I get to college they can send for an ambulance."

And this became the goal. It never occurred to me to sit down and dial 999. I could die alone waiting for help to come.

I picked up my jacket and my briefcase - heaven knows why – and somehow got the car out of the garage. I was sweating profusely. Then I decided I could not make college and far more sensible to drive round to the doctor's surgery.

I don't really remember the drive. Oh yes, the bloody milk float nearly blocked me in and I had to manoeuvre between it and the wall. .

"Typical. You're dying and the milkman calls."

Then again, the street outside the surgery was full and I had to drive halfway up Lime Grove to park.

The walk back to the surgery was an ordeal, but the door was still open and, miraculously it seemed, I could see Doctor Sherski in the reception.

I had to hold myself up on the doorjamb. I waited politely. He was talking to his wife I believe. Then he saw me.

"Are you alright?" I probably looked terrible. I told him I had pains in my chest and arms and he waved me into his surgery.

The predictable questions, the blood pressure, the stethoscope bit and he got me down on the couch.

"Just a pin-prick. This will ease the pain." I believe he gave me another injection then, this time in my thigh. Whether from the injection, or what, I was only half with the scene by now. He was fussing around behind me somewhere.

2

"I'm not sure whether it is a heart attack or not, but we must not take the chance and I'd like to get you into hospital as soon as possible. I have sent for an ambulance."

That sounded alright with me. I could not think of a better place to be at that moment.

"Could you please ring Sandra and tell her?" I felt very anxious that he should do this while I could still remember her number. But he had to do something else first and I began to get bothered. I kept rehearsing her telephone number in my mind in case I forgot it.

It seemed an age but was probably only a moment before he asked me for Sandra's number. He then left me alone in his surgery, presumably to make the call. I remember him coming back to say that he had spoken to her, but the sedation was making me feel quite detached by now because I took the information for granted.

Things had become distinctly woozy. There is a blur of ambulance men, a wheelchair, a vivid red blanket, a pair of shoes in my lap on the blanket and then the surprising lightness inside the ambulance.

I have a hazy vision of houses and cars through the windows and of a drive which seemed to last for ever. And then I was being carried into the hospital. A very young girl is looking into my eyes and I sense a great feeling of compassion. She says she is a doctor and there follows more questions, more injections and numerous wires to my chest, plus a drip into my wrist. But it is all a bit remote, half real and half as if observed, like a familiar scene on the tele. They must have undressed me at some stage for later that day I became aware that I only had my pants on. A comment and not a concern. Hell, I couldn't care less what I had on - or off.

3

That was Casualty and the next thing I became aware of was being wheeled along corridors which consisted visually of only ceiling and ceiling lights. The driving was at best indifferent, as I felt obliged to fend off doors as we rumbled through them. A vast lift which took the bed, the porters, the mobile drip and a few spectators as well; more corridors and we had arrived somewhere. Intensive Care. It had to be. I recognised the high tech, the oscilloscopes, the observation screen and the numerous nurses beyond.

I think the first thing they did after plugging me in was to write up my inventory. This appears to be top priority in any Intensive Care, vital to survival. Perhaps it is designed almost to trivialise the reason why you are there - the heart attack - or whatever. My clothes were produced, pockets emptied and the contents carefully noted. A wallet, pen, pencil, comb and 57p in small change. My large Seiko wrist watch - waterproof down to 150 metres - was thoughtfully put back on to my *right* wrist, while the rest of my possessions were put into a large brown envelope. I was then given a copy of the inventory, although God knows where I could have put it. Sandra said later that she was given my clothes, all carefully screwed up and stuffed into a very large red plastic bag labelled 'Patients Property'.

When one thinks of hospitals one thinks of medication, treatment, perhaps surgery and of course nursing. But such mundane things as the security of the patient's belongings have also to be designed for. It is not all bedpans and pills.

Lying, half propped, in Intensive Care I was happy not to be able to see the electronic display behind the bed. I was only too aware of my irregular heartbeats without seeing them depicted on screen. I was also immensely thankful that there was no audible bleep to accompany the screen trace.

Sandra arrived at half past two. She was worried sick but did her best to hide it. I was so glad to see her. I hated the way she kept staring at the oscilloscope behind me and I told her to stop looking at it. It was obviously mesmeric. I could just see it by peering over my shoulder. I was just in time to see something that looked like a starburst amongst the irregular peaks. I resolved never to look at it again.

My nephew Michael arrived a bit later and he too sat staring at the bloody screen. I cannot recall our conversation. I think I was sedated because it was very difficult to stay awake and I kept floating away. At some stage a doctor examined me and asked even more questions. I think he drew off some blood samples as well. Whatever he did, or anyone else for that matter, made little impact upon my awareness. I was definitely not tuned into the scene and hence not as worried about myself as I could have been. Sandra and Michael both left at about four o'clock. Their plan apparently was to recover the car from where I had left it as Sandra was obviously going to need it, and to make a few phone calls.

They returned in about an hour or so, bringing me some pyjamas and toilet things and Michael left again at six. He found my son at the lift looking for me and he brought him back to the ward. Jonathan was subdued and without his usual funnies. I don't suppose I was a bundle of laughs either. They said afterwards that I looked a 'sort of grey-yellow'.

Small talk in such circumstances does not flow freely and in the absence of any other topic they had to zone in upon the blasted oscilloscope display. There were four screens I think and each one showing a different feature, just like BBC and ITV. All live broadcasts and I hoped they kept that way.

They all went at about eight o'clock, leaving me feeling not too uncomfortable with just a slight pain in my chest like indigestion. I guess I dozed on and off thereafter through the night.

DAY TWO

It was not a good night, in fact. I kept surfacing from sleep feeling less and less comfortable. The indigestion pain was increasing and by five o'clock when a very young and new nurse came in I felt very unhappy. She propped me up a little higher to mark the transition from hospital night to day and I immediately felt very sick.

She only just managed to get a basin under my chin before I spewed. The poor girl was nearly as unhappy as I was. She held the basin at arms length, pleading with me not to strain. I brought up what looked like half a pint of black coffee grounds; she told me it was stale blood. Now that worried me. What the hell had that to do with a heart attack?

I thought about the indigestion pains and decided that was what they were about. When the doctor appeared a bit later to draw off some more blood from my arm, I told him how I thought I had a hiatus hernia and would that account for the internal bleeding? He replied by taking an extra phial of blood saying, "We need to test for your blood type - in case we have to give you a transfusion." I could do without this, I thought. He did explain something about a heart attack being a massive shock to the system and how it could well pop an ulcer.

I certainly could not face food in any shape or form. They tried me on a few dishes, a bowl of soup and a sandwich, but these made me feel like spewing again. It was about this time that I sensed a vaguely growing suspicion that it might not have been a heart attack after all. The doctor explained that they needed the results of blood tests taken over three days to be sure one way or the other.

It had been an eventful morning.

Sandra arrived at eleven. She had not had a very good night either, I guess, poor girl. I can imagine how I would have felt had the boot been on the other foot. She said the telephone had not stopped ringing all evening. Jonathan arrived a bit later bringing me a stack of yachting and motoring magazines, bless him. He had taken the day off work.

It seemed to be a good sign that they intend to move me up to a general medical ward this evening. That could only be good news we thought. Sandra and Jonathan went off for lunch at one o'clock and Sandra returned promptly an hour later. Then at about five there was a hustle of porters and I was trundled off up to the sixth floor to the Brunswick ward.

Only four of its six beds were occupied and I was lifted by one nurse and two porters from the Intensive Care bed on to the ward bed. This was not a good move. Lying back on pillows on a flat sheet of metal is preferable to lying on pillows on iron rods at six-inch centres. As if this inept bit of design were not bad enough, the bed then has to have a sheet of plastic over the mattress, presumably to ensure that one doesn't pee on it. Unfortunately this is also a sweat barrier and the crisp cotton sheet on which one is lying soon becomes horribly cold and damp. You try alternating from one side of the bed to the other to allow each half to dry out in turn. Then I later used my bath towel for additional insulation from the plastic. Why should sick people have to suffer a preventable inconvenience like this? It cannot be beyond the wit of someone to come up with an absorbent material which, although lined one side, is still launderable. I was not the only one to suffer from this and I did hear other patients complain about lying on sweat-wet sheets.

My bed was the corner one, directly beneath the window. It had a superb view south over most of Kingston. Not a little time was occupied identifying buildings and places. How immensely important is a view like that to the bedridden and to people generally in that sort of situation. I could see the tower block on the Knights Park campus and could almost see my office window.

I discovered the snag with this bed position as soon as the sun got round to its afternoon place. It beat in and started cooking me pink. I eventually moved to a bed at the other end of the ward, but that was only a couple of days before I left the hospital. Meanwhile I enjoyed the view and put up with the cooking.

I had a portable oscilloscope this time, although no one ever looked at it. After having been bedded in and Sandra had rejoined me, the Staff Nurse introduced herself - Cheryl. She was one of the super ones, compassionate and immensely professional. She gave us a detailed and very clear explanation of what a heart attack is and how it is treated. The heart muscle needs oxygen and this is supplied by the coronary arteries which surround the heart. If this oxygen supply is cut off at any time by, say, a restriction in one of these arteries blocking the blood flow, that bit of the heart served by that artery dies. That is when one feels the pain and why it used to be called a coronary thrombosis. Today it is popularly called a heart attack, or more properly, myocardial infarction - myo meaning muscles, cardial meaning heart and infarction the change the damaged area of the heart undergoes.

The really critical period is the couple of days following the attack. After that every day that passes reduces the risk of something dire happening. The bit of the heart that dies then gives off enzymes which are detectable in the blood. The amount of these enzymes present gives the clue as to the scale of the attack. A few enzymes would indicate a mild attack, whereas a massive attack would produce many enzymes. Cheryl said that the results of yesterday's test on my blood were clear, no enzymes! I immediately felt much better. Could it be that I had not had an attack? She said it was possible but that tests done over three days were necessary to be absolutely certain.

I was very reassured by this conversation which, either way, removed many questions from my mind. I even nibbled at the steak and kidney pie served for dinner. Jonathan came back again and sat by the bedside, to be followed shortly by Michael. Everyone said how much better I now looked. The ward seemed to be full of visitors and activity. The bell went at eight o'clock when they all disappeared. I had begun to feel a bit overwhelmed and the sudden hush was very welcome.

I had not peed since yesterday morning and I thought I should try. So I asked for a bottle and managed it with difficulty leaning over the side of the bed.

With all of the visitors gone I could now review my fellow patients. The bed opposite was empty but next to it was an elderly man called Henry. He did not seem to be very ill and was sitting out in his pyjamas. A comfortably rounded midriff strained this garment to near indecency. Henry was a retired plasterer, a man with great wisdom and yet much humility. Pneumonia had brought him in and a persisting chest infection stopped him from going out. He was a listener and everyone else in the ward talked to him with their troubles and Henry always told them in reply what they wanted to hear. He was spiritually in charge of the ward although he would have been

9

the last one to know this. His mobility enabled him to fetch and carry for everyone else.

Predictably, Henry did not at first like his neighbour, Edward. "Nothing in common there," said quite openly and honestly. He in fact changed his mind completely before he left. Edward did come over as a very old and very irascible gentleman. He had fallen and fractured vertebrae in his spine. He was in constant severe pain and at that stage quite immobile. He coughed and wheezed alarmingly and snored fit to awaken the dead.

Opposite Edward was Stan, also an elderly retired gentleman who had a mysterious pain in his shoulder which they could not diagnose. He too was mobile. He and Henry had a great deal in common; they talked endlessly, either at their bedsides or from one end of the ward to the other, from five in the morning to midnight. I detected this duo as a likely future problem, particularly as their conversation was predictable and boring.

The final member of Brunswick was Bert. Now Bert was a sad sort of figure. His wife had died five years ago and one got the impression that Bert could not wait to join her. It was a constant theme he returned to in every conversation. A neighbour had found him a couple of days previously, lying on his back with his eyes wide open, but out to the world. They were going to send him off somewhere to do a brain scan. "Not me," and he would go through the motions of drilling. "Hm ... Sawdust." Meanwhile, Bert dithered. He dithered, demurred and apologized constantly.

The ward regime appeared to be relaxed. The lights went out when everyone was ready, except for Henry's and he carried on reading until ten thirty. Then he and Stan carried on talking until eleven. I regretted not taking a sleeping pill when offered on the evening drugs round.

DAY THREE

It is five o'clock and Stan and Henry are still talking! I do not believe it. They could well have been talking all night, but mercifully I must have slept. I tried hard to escape to sleep again and probably did doze on and off, but the ward finally won at about seven with the first drugs round.

Medicine is dispensed three times daily and with curious formality. Two nurses wheel a large encased trolley with a hinged and lockable lid into the ward. It contains numerous bottles of pills, potions, tablets and whatever, which the two nurses dispense with immense care and consultation, after reference to each patient's chart hanging from the bed ends. One nurse, usually Staff, pours, counts, or measures the relevant amount of medication into a plastic beaker, in front of the nose of the second nurse, who then ritualistically checks this dose off against the prescription on the chart once again. The ritual is then completed by giving the medicine to the patient, who has to swallow it before the nurse moves on to the next bed. I failed to swallow a dose once and it was discovered later on the edge of my locker. A nurse then lectured me very seriously about how I had created an 'unprotected drugs area' and how this could get the nurse into very deep trouble.

The day-team of nurses arrives at half past nine and they usually breeze into the ward to say good morning. One scans them anxiously to see if one's favourites are on duty. The team seems to consist of a Sister, who is in charge of the ward and recognised by her royal blue uniform, a couple of Staff Nurses in white uniforms and dark green epaulettes, and four, or so, student nurses. These latter do all the work, of course, and are dressed in blue and white check uniforms with one, two, or three stripes on their caps, denoting First, Second, or Third Year students. Knowing about this hierarchy amongst the

11

nurses is important for the patient. He has to know both how and who to ask for things like baths, bottles or bedpans. A First Year student can give you a bottle, but it takes Sister to agree to a bath. Thank God I never had to use a bedpan!

Ward routine ensures that the patient never gets bored. The morning, from seven onwards, seems filled with busy to-ing and fro-ing. First, the blood pressure, pulse and temperature bit, followed closely by the drugs round and then breakfast. One is then encouraged to wash, be washed - bath, be bathed - or allowed to pass, depending upon your state of health. That first morning in the ward, I was surprised to find that I could wash myself. I happily agreed, but said I thought I should try to use a bedpan, or something, first. I had not been to the loo for a couple of days and this was beginning to preoccupy me. I did not fancy it one bit. This is where the importance of knowing about nurse hierarchy comes in. Had I asked this of a student nurse I am sure I would have had the unpleasantness of a bed pan and all the embarrassment, to me, of dealing with it and its proceeds. As it was, Staff Nurse Cheryl popped me on to a mobile commode, wheeled me to the ward loo and left me to it. She did tell me not to strain and to take my time. How civilized. I shat more black coffee grounds!

I told myself that this was the original lot going through me and that as I had not had any more indigestion pains it need not still be bleeding. I told Cheryl and she noted it on my chart.

My wash-down, sitting on the edge of the bed, was very enjoyable, the first for two days. So it made me puff, but I felt a bit more fragrant.

The final event of the morning was Doctors' Rounds. These involve either the Houseman, Dr Kerr, known to all the nurses, no matter how junior, as Kate, or the Houseman and the Registrar, Dr Gunraj, or the really big scene when the first two accompany the consultant, Dr Knowles. I only ever saw the Big Man once, although he was written down on everything as my doctor.

This morning it was just Kate. She was the one who greeted me on arrival in Casualty, the one with the compassionate eyes. I liked her. She reminded me a lot of some of my own postgraduate students. Lots of excellent theory, often beyond my comprehension, but short of the experience needed to make the theory work. I was probably doing her an awful injustice. Anyway, I was to lose a lot of my enthusiasm for her following her news. She told me that the second blood test had been positive and that the presence of enzymes showed that I had indeed had a heart attack. The news depressed me immensely. I had not realized how much I had been banking upon the doubts previously raised. Perhaps I had misread what they had said, but I had really begun to think it was simply my ulcer playing up. If I had not misread them then they had been very naughty in building up my hopes.

I began to feel ill once more.

Kate launched into her post-heart-attack-information spiel. It struck me that this was a standard speech and I suppose that was in itself reassuring. She made it sound commonplace.

By the time Sandra arrived at half past two, I had recovered somewhat, although the news did surprise her also, confirming my impression that they had mistakenly built up our hopes. Staff Nurse Cheryl brought us some pamphlets published by the British Heart Foundation. One of these, Back to Normal, was very helpful, full of convincing encouragement, advice and reassurance. We read it and felt a bit better.

Edward's wife had arrived and we became aware at this stage of some problem at that end of the ward. They had obviously lost something. Mrs Edward, who was called Margaret incidentally, had gone somewhere and a nurse was moving things about, around Edward, as he sat up in bed. "What's that?" She moved the locker. "What?" "By the skirting." She moved the other locker. "A tooth brush." "It's not mine," said Edward, "Mine's in my locker." "What did you see then?" "I don't know what I saw." "Where?" "To the left there." She put the toothbrush carefully into the locker she had just moved and peered closely to the left of it. She pounced. "It's a sweet."

Margaret came in. A tall, slim, elegant woman. "What are you looking for?" The nurse told her. Edward cupped his ear in his hand. "What are you looking for?" "YOUR HEARING AID!" she bellowed.

Peter arrived later in the evening from the Polytechnic and brought a large get-well-soon card, signed by all the staff in Architecture and the Faculty office. He said that the staff in the library, when they heard of a card, had all trooped down to sign it. There were about forty messages and signatures on it, including a composite one telephoned from the School of Law at Gipsy Hill. I particularly liked the one from my secretary, "Get a grip on yourself!" Another one admonished me with, "Stop that malingering!!"and others including, "What an extremely silly thing to do!"... "Come back soon - everyone is fighting over your parking space."... "Academic Board wasn't that bad"... "A masterly concept - Wimbledon, or the Test Match?"

Both Peter and Michael, when he arrived, said that they could not walk down the corridor at college without being stopped every yard or so by people asking about me. It is a great lift to one's morale to know that people are thinking

14

about you like that. I felt very grateful to everyone who sent me their love and good wishes.

Peter said that the Director had told him he would call to see me tomorrow evening. Bob had telephoned Sandra the evening it had happened.

That evening I had Sandra, Jonathan, Michael and Peter around the bed and at one stage I began to feel overwhelmed. It was all getting too much for me, as they say. A girl came into the ward, going from bed to bed, inviting record requests to be played on the Hospital Radio this evening. I asked for Mozart's 21st Piano Concerto. A likely one, I thought. But they actually played it ... "And now for something completely different," he said. My fellow patients were charmed and Henry said that he would sleep all the better for having listened to it. As lullabies go Mozart must score over Madonna!

The night shift took over at half past nine and bedded us down after the evening drugs round. Henry said he hoped I would not keep them all awake tonight with my snoring ... "As you did last night". Stan agreed with him. And they were the two who talked all night long!

DAY FOUR

The sun has shone and the weather has been beautiful since I came into hospital. Summer 1987 was a long time a'coming, but here in July it seems to have arrived. If the days are hot, the nights in Brunswick are cold. The cool night air washes down from the windows in sharp contrast with the heat of the day and my bed position beneath the windows receives both of these extremes. I sweat in the day and shiver at night. Although I had slept well I had been cold and decided that I would ask for a blanket.

I seem to be the last to wake up in the morning. By six o'clock everyone is chattering away, the nurses are abustle and I am still trying to doze deep in the covers. I am defeated at seven when the blood pressure round starts. Thereafter, one resigns and slides up the pillows to join the rest of the world.

The tea trolley is another minor event which occurs at regular intervals. I say 'tea trolley' when in fact it also serves coffee, chocolate and Bovril. On one occasion it served all four at the same time. Henry was the choked recipient.

Although visiting does not start until half past two, Sandra popped in just before eight, to bring me my slippers. Paddling around in the loo in bare feet, where the aim of some of my colleagues is not all it should be, is not on. She brought them into the ward rather guiltily and was backing out again when Sister stopped her. "You're not going so soon?"

Sister was quite happy to ignore the rules, but Sandra actually wanted to do the weekend shopping before spending the rest of the day with me.

Drugs, breakfast, loo, wash, all follow in an orderly fashion, with the loo bit only being remarkable. I passed more coffee grounds, but I guess this could still be the original lot going through - I tell myself.

Doctors' Rounds this morning is the big one. Dr Knowles, the Consultant, is due although this did not seem to create the fuss I expected it to. Perhaps I was thinking of the Carry on Doctor series. Anyway, reminiscent of James Robertson Justice, Dr Knowles was accompanied by the Sister, the Houseman (Houseperson?) and the Registrar. Consultation is behind drawn curtains each time and I could not quite hear the whispered conversation before they came through the curtains. He confirmed the heart attack and said that I was coming along nicely. He questioned me about my ulcer, but

16

said they could do nothing about that yet until my heart had settled down. He then told me that he wanted me to sit out of bed for half an hour this afternoon, for an hour on Saturday and three hours, or so, on Sunday. Then if I could walk up two flights of stairs without any pain, I could go home on Tuesday. It sounded marvellous.

I asked him what had actually happened. I told him that it had been a very quiet morning, no physical or emotional stress, and suddenly I had a heart attack. Why? He said that it was not what I had been doing at the time, but rather what I had done over the last thirty years. There is no answer to that.

I was delighted to see my ex-Faculty Administrative Officer hobbling into the ward, just before lunch - delighted to see him, that is. Graham Bennett had smashed his kneecap playing tennis and was attending hospital for physiotherapy. He looked more like a patient than many of us inmates, with his leg in plaster from ankle to groin. Graham is now Assistant Academic Registrar, a very worthy promotion. He is the best administrator I have ever known, probably because he brings to the job the most advanced sense of anti-bullshit I have ever had the joy to observe. His skill at pricking the pompous, or deriding the self-important, is devastating and as a source of gossip he is without equal. True to form, he gave me the advance notice of Liz Esteve-Cole's appointment as Director of the V and A Museum. Liz was our Librarian and only left two or three years ago to take over the V and A Library. She was a smashing girl and used to fight her corner with terrific zest. Good for the Victoria and Albert.

When she arrived at half past two Sandra was delighted to hear the news that I should be able to go home on Tuesday and we read through all the leaflets once again to check what I should be doing once I get home. They make a great thing about depression and the need to think positively. Apparently, one can be quite scared about leaving the hospital when that time comes and about being left alone. One feels very vulnerable.

Bert left us this afternoon in much confusion on his part. The doctor told him that he was to be taken to another hospital for a brain scan and that although he would be brought back to Kingston he could go home thereafter. Henry explained this to him afterwards at least three times, but Bert never really understood what was to happen. He did come back again during the evening and fussed around his locker and then disappeared, without saying a word to anyone.

Stan also left after lunch. Handshakes all round. A bit like the end of session really. It is strange how people take on a different persona once they dress up in their day clothes. Stan looked much younger in his crisp white shirt and dark suit.

So we have lost two of our brethren, but we gained one this morning. He is about thirty and has a thick Scottish brogue. They put him in the bed opposite me and he appears to be completely paralyzed. He groans and moans whenever anyone tries to move him. He asks constantly for painkillers, but the nurses explained they could not give him anything without the doctor's authority. This battle over painkillers developed as more and more nurses were badgered by him. It does seem very odd that something cannot be done and Henry is getting quite upset about it.

"I've got a son your age and I wouldn't want to see him suffer like this."

I believe Henry did speak to Cheryl, because he told us later that the new patient is bogus. Apparently he was admitted on Monday, sent to the Atkinson Morley Hospital for

18

tests, including a lumbar puncture, and they could find nothing wrong with him. He claims that he is chronically semi-paralysed and that periodically he becomes acutely paralysed. I heard the physiotherapist say to him, "How can you say you are paralysed when your arm muscles are so firm and healthy?." He certainly looks very robust and fit. Yet he finishes each one of these exchanges snivelling, "I've had enough of this, I cannot take much more." But even this sounds more in anger than despair.

All of the nurses have had a go at him and each time it has finished in the same way. His dinner was presented up to him, but he claimed that he could not feed himself. Eventually a nurse fed him, but with little grace. She maintained a conversation across the ward with me, rather than talk to him. I wonder what is the truth? Is he bogus, or is it a psychopathic condition and if so why do they not treat him accordingly? He claims that he has come down from Edinburgh and had been staying with his girl friend when this developed. They asked if they should get in touch with her, but he did not want them to. Henry's sympathy has diminished by now and I noticed him sitting on the other side of the bed, facing away from him.

After the visitors had gone and the ward regime had recovered, Staff and her nurse aide warned us about the night shift. Tonight we will meet Ann Elizabeth! She was given a tremendous introduction which variously had her as beautiful, a harridan, Irish, tough, sweet and a card. The emphasis though was upon her Irish beauty. This made Henry very suspicious and he speculated upon a twenty-stone Trinidadian, with a temper to match. We all tended to agree.

At half past nine the drugs trolley went past the end of the ward, pushed by ... a twenty-stone black girl!

It was a false alarm however, because a bit later this beautiful, sky-blue-eyed blonde breezed in like a spring storm. She went round the ward in a blur of activity keeping up a constant flow of patter as she worked. Within a few minutes the ward was immaculate, chairs in place, curtains pulled, bottles distributed, the television unplugged and against the wall, lockers tidied and empty cups collected. It was the most professional exhibition of efficiency I saw in that hospital.

Her patter was hilarious. She cracked a funny at every patient. "Berry? I know a lot of Berrys in Ireland. They are all Knackers. Berry the Tinker, Berry the Taylor. All Knackers." It sounded very insulting although not meant that way I'm sure.

"Come on now Mr Bates. You are not here to enjoy yourself."

"Move over there now Henry, let me get into bed with you," and she lay on the bed beside Henry with her arm around his neck. Henry, rising to the occasion, said, "I've got a headache."

Each one of these nurses brings something different to a hospital ward. I am not sure that Ann Elizabeth's contribution was universally appropriate for all patients. Something a little gentler is my preference, someone like Cheryl perhaps?

DAY FIVE

Thank heavens, my bowel movement this morning was normal. For the first time I have not passed blood. So that merely leaves the heart attack!

The third Test match started on Thursday and of course this is the final week at Wimbledon. There is a television set in the ward, but until now I had not felt much compulsion to watch it. Henry had been the only other one interested in cricket, so

20

he had organised the set so that we could both see it. Thursday had been pretty disastrous when Pakistan bowled us out for peanuts, Imran Khan doing it all. And then they went in and showed us what an easy wicket it was, or how strokes should be played. The nurses couldn't care less about the cricket and were constantly asking for Wimbledon. Henry did his best to share things out between us, but at times got himself hooked on the tennis. Not that it really mattered; the cricket was depressing anyway. Out of deference to everyone else he kept the sound turned right down, so that one lost the thread if you stopped watching.

It was the men's' finals today and the nurses, who all seemed to be rooting for Cash, were more demanding than ever. So we did not see much cricket anyway.

I was beginning to have shouted conversations with Edward by now, from one end of the ward to the other. He was still without his hearing aid. He read 'Greats' at Oxford and that must have been around about the depression in the 'twenties. What a time to try and make sense of life. He asked me which university I was at? Architecture was not a good university subject when I was a student and I told him I was at the Leicester College of Art and Technology. It must have sounded like an apology and I only just stopped myself from adding - "I'm afraid." He took it as an apology anyway. "Ah well, they are all places of learning." he said.

"Can't someone move these two next to each other? The whole bloody hospital can hear them." That comment, I believe from Henry, did prompt me to ask if my bed could be moved to the other end and not just to make conversation with Edward easier, but to escape from the sun as well.

The nurses were still having problems with our paralysed friend, although Tracy, a Third Year, was being extremely patient. She spent some time talking with him and eventually went off and got the mobile public telephone. He made a call to his girl friend and I could not help overhearing most of his conversation. It was pure fantasy. He told her how they were still giving him tests and were going to move him into a private ward - the better to observe him. The sequel to this event happened in the evening when he demanded to be fed once again. Staff Nurse told him that as he was observed holding a telephone without effort, he could now try holding a spoon.

Henry's wife had brought his clothes in last night and he was due to be collected after lunch today. He dressed himself slowly, but full of complaint. "Fancy bringing my winter suit in on a day like this." It was a broiling hot day, up in the nineties. He telephoned home and I heard him open the conversation, "I still wear pants, you know."

Edward and I were genuinely sorry to see Henry go. He had been through the Desert Campaign, "Although I never got above corporal." The salt of the earth, as they say!

Talking of clichés, it is a cliché to talk about the patience of nurses, but while most of them are divine, some are simply thick. They decided that Edward needed a shave. The hospital razor was produced. It did not work. Edward has a razor, so Tracy got it from his locker. She could not make Edward's razor work either. Perhaps it was just Tracy. Then the Scottish lad wanted the telephone. She dropped the razor and went off to collect the mobile unit, plugging it in appropriately. Then she had to dial the number for him, having first scrounged 10p pieces from everyone.

Back to the razor and Edward, but he was now complaining heavily of a pain in his right testicle. I believe he has a bedsore there. "I've been trying to get my 'little man' out."

"Do you want a bottle?" Tracy asked him. "No. That's where the pain is." Tracy wandered off, tossing the razor from hand to hand. She came back in a few minutes still tossing the razor. It was the hospital razor again. She plugged it in and it buzzed furiously in her hand. The head dropped off.

It was like a badly written farce, all very predictable and acted out so carefully. The next scene opens with Tracy giving the razor to a male student nurse. Now, he was a thick one. He suggests that poor, patient Edward shaves himself. Edward declines and in response to the male nurse's insistence, tells him he is too involved with pain to think about shaving. It sounded a convincing argument to me and I could see his point. Not so the male nurse. "That's a good excuse, ha ha." No, definitely not divine this one and Edward never did get his shave.

Michael and Sue Blackstock came during the afternoon and I entertained them from a chair by the bedside. They were going on to a barbecue at Steyning later. It was a gorgeous sunny evening and I suddenly felt very envious. The world intruded upon me for the first time.

Jonathan came in quite late, still with grease traces on his hands and arms from his car. He had been working on it all day.

They moved me up to the other end of the ward in the evening and moved the Scottish lad out to another ward altogether. I must say I was not sorry. Edward and I now had the ward to ourselves. With Margaret visiting Edward and Sandra sitting with me, we were quite a cosy little party. We had the television up between us, although Margaret was more interested in the cricket than Edward was. Not that anyone was very interested, England were back at the crease and looked as ineffectual as they did in their first innings. I had to think what marvellously strong hearts these chaps must have, pounding up and down the wicket like that all day.

We were not to be in sole occupancy for long, because they brought a young fellow in who looked a bit like Anthony Newley and who apparently was suffering from heat stroke. He only spent the night with us and was discharged the following day.

A lovely young Jamaican girl came on duty that evening. I had not seen her before and I believe she was an agency nurse. She came and talked to me for an hour or so and I found myself giving her a career tutorial. She was State Registered and had done Midwifery and was now thinking of doing something completely different. She was keen to do some sort of social welfare work. I did my best to dissuade her, thinking of the frustrating and unrewarding life a friend of mine suffers in such a career, not from the work itself, but from the inhibiting bureaucracy behind the work. I suggested psychology and recommended the range of such courses the Open University offers. The idea appealed to her as one which would not be too dramatic a change of path.

It made me feel half useful once more.

DAY SIX

"There are some bodily functions I don't mind doing in public."

"Like what?"

"I don't mind eating in public, but I hate having to pee like this."

I suppose one would get indifferent eventually to the sight of an elderly gentleman, hunched over, with a cardboard 'bottle' clutched up to his crotch, wearing that vacant expression that goes with urination. It is not an everyday sight, except in these places, of course.

"I wouldn't want to copulate in public either."

"I don't think I could."

He thought on it for a moment. "A bit like peeing really."

Edward was something in the Board of Trade during the war - 'Petroleum Statistics' I believe. Harold Wilson was there also, at that time, working on coal statistics. Edward said that although Harold was a self-confessed Liberal, he told him that he intended to enter politics as a Socialist. "The Labour Party is the one which will pick up the young voter after the war." Edward thought this was very amoral, "Typical of the man!"

He spoke disparagingly of Barbara Castle too, or at least said his wife did. She apparently knew her and "They did not get along at all well." I can imagine a strong personality conflict between them. Margaret came through, on the short acquaintance of visiting hours, as a very forthright and quite delightful lady and one of tremendous character. I do not know Barbara Castle, but I think one could well describe her in similar terms.

The ladies singles final starts at half past two. No one seems to want Navratilova to win. One of the nurses thought she should be playing in the men's' final. We got the television organized in the aisle between our beds ready for the event. There is no cricket on today, so I am content to capitulate over which channel we watch. Our visitors arrived at half past two and the heat-stroke lad was joined by his wife and a very new baby.

The hospital patient's social behaviour can cynically be said to be largely influenced by the survival instinct. If you help your fellow patient you hope he will help you reciprocally. In this way you try to build up a little credit against the day when you will need help yourself. The normal self-survival instinct which might curb this apparently altruistic behaviour is therefore somewhat suppressed and people appear to be much less self-centred than otherwise. It is a bit like the old wartime spirit - uniting against the common enemy - which in the hospital ward must be fear and pain.

But of course there is always the odd man out, the one whose confidence has not been shattered by some unexpected calamity and who is obviously looking after number one first, last, and in the middle. He moved into the ward today. They brought his portable tele in with him, a mini computer and a transistor radio - with earphones, thank God. He was immediately on about getting into one of the adjoining single wards. He does not appear to be desperately ill, just passing blood I believe. But who doesn't? That is the point, I guess, he does not feel threatened. He can indulge his basic self-centeredness without feeling the need for a bit of protective insurance. He wears a sweatshirt and shorts and is on a mobile drip, which means that he can push this contraption around the ward with him and into the loo.

The food is worthy of comment, mostly good. A large, blonde lady, an auxiliary of some sort in a pink uniform, brings the menu cards around periodically and one ticks off the dishes one wants. Breakfast consists of a choice of cereals, or fruit juice, followed by boiled or scrambled egg, or sausages and tomatoes. The whole-wheat bread and marmalade sounds great, except that it is the wrapped-sliced variety which disintegrates under the butter and the marmalade. The choice is limited, but the scrambled egg is just like home cooking. Lunch always consists of a choice of three or four main dishes, preceded by soup and followed by pudding. My lunches included roast beef with a commendable Yorkshire pud, lamb and mint sauce, steak and kidney pie, fried cod and a stuffed pimento. Not exactly haute cuisine, but very good canteen fodder. Supper, so-called, was also a hot main course and pudding. It was too much to eat two main meals a day when one was not burning it off with lots of exercise, so I usually had just a bowl of soup and a sandwich for supper. These were very tasty, including tuna and salad, cheese and pickle, cold beef and so on. I got into the ritual of marking up everyone's menu card, which as far as Edward was concerned, meant making the choice for him as well. He had not enjoyed the food up to this time, but he obviously approved of my selections, because he thought the food had suddenly improved.

I was pottering around the ward by now, making excursions to the window and back and peeping out of the ward at the other ones adjoining. Pioneering stuff. I discovered that our team of nurses were in fact dealing with about twenty patients altogether in three six-bed wards and a few single isolation wards. The other couple of six-bed wards were female. My previous excursion into hospital, a brief one, was to St George's where the wards were mixed. This seemed wholly unremarkable at the time and very pleasant. Here at Kingston, the notion of mixing the sexes in the wards leaves the nurses falling about.

The women's final seemed a dull event to me, all over in three sets. Navratilova vanquished the much more feminine German girl, to everyone's regret, but a British mixed doubles pair won the next final, which was a much more popular result.

A nurse came in to tell me that my son was on the phone to speak to me. I took the call out at the nurses' station. This was quite irregular of course, but Jonathan thought they transferred calls to the patients by means of the mobile trolley. He had been working on his car all day and had left it too late to visit.

I carried on watching the television after Sandra had left, a sign that I must have been feeling better. She rang the ward every night I was in hospital, at about ten, to ask the nurse to say goodnight to me and again every morning at seven to ask what sort of night I had had. The nurse would sometimes stand at the entrance and call out, "That was your wife Mr Berry, to say that she loves you." Henry said once, "What a lovely girl. You are a lucky chap Dennis." That I know!

The peace of the ward was jarred later that evening when two new patients were wheeled in. This happened quite late and we gathered that it was something of an emergency. They had to move these two patients from the single wards into our ward, to enable the single wards to become isolation units. The nurses had to wear special gowns, facemasks and gloves whenever they subsequently entered these units, a time-consuming process which added to their normal burdens.

DAY SEVEN

Well, it's all go. The two new patients they brought in last night were wheeled out again this morning to make room for another two new patients, and alas, the Scottish lad has turned up again. They are shuttling him around like a coal truck in a siding. So the ward is once more full.

The poor old chap next to Edward is on oxygen all the time and struggling to breathe. The other new one, again an elderly man, lies there quite inert and uncommunicative.

If I am to go home tomorrow I have to pass the staircase test today. I am quite apprehensive about this because so far I have only pottered slowly around the ward and even that has made me puff. I was lying on my bed, gathering strength, when the staff nurse came in and said the time had come. She walked me smartly out of the ward in search of the staircase always about three steps in front of me like a women taking out her reluctant dog. Along the corridor, around the corner, through the doors and I begin to wonder if I will survive the quest for the staircase, let alone climb it. Finally we make the stairs and she introduces me to them like mien host at a party.

"Mr Berry, this is the staircase." I wait for her to say, "Staircase, this is Mr Berry"... but she does not share my fantasy.

The stairs have ten steps in each flight and she then tells me I have to walk up two flights. I tell her not to be silly. It was as much as I could do to walk up two flights of stairs when I was fit! But she insists, so I set out to prove her wrong. Amazingly, I climbed both flights and walked back to the ward without any problems. I have no pains and everyone is delighted. So, great news for Sandra when she arrives.

Edward said that his daughter, called Tinkle, was visiting this afternoon. She got her name as a baby when she called her pot 'tinkle'. This was derived from the sound she made peeing into it. Tinkle turned out to be a younger replica of her mother, the same delightful attitude and zest for life and slightly larger than life. Although about fifty years old she came over as a young woman of thirty. Edward said that as a young girl she was courted by three lads, one of whom has maintained a friendship with her to this day. His name is John Biffen, the man recently relegated to the backbenches in Margaret Thatcher's cabinet reshuffle, following her re-election for the third term.

John Biffen and Michael Heseltine, also of the backbenches, are said to be keeping closely in touch with each other. While Heseltine has the support in the constituencies, Biffen has the support in the House. So presumably they must represent some sort of collective power and one wonders to what end they might use it? It would be a marvellous thing for this country, I believe, if there were to be some major realignment of the right resulting in a strengthening of the centre affinities and a halting of the present tendency towards political polarity. What sort of choice is it between Marxism and Fascism, for that is what we seem to be moving towards sometimes?

Meanwhile the Test Match is resumed - and finished - ingloriously. England was beaten by an innings and umpteen runs. There was little entertainment in the watching, but it did invoke Edward to question the quirk of human nature which makes us goggle at sport on the box so obsessively. Why do we get so passionate about Wimbledon, the Test Match, Wembley, or go off in our millions every Saturday to watch the local team? What is it about watching two men (women?) hitting a ball at each other over a net? What makes a spectator sport - athleticism, dexterity, competitiveness, professionalism? All of these no doubt, plus many other factors.

We can all admire someone performing skilfully and with professional application, like a racing driver, or a Centre Court performer at Wimbledon. But I can never understand the enrapt audience at a chess tournament? The skill here is mental and thus unobservable, other than in its effect and the competition is implicit rather than explicit. Dexterity is zero and athleticism is non-existent. So what grabs the audience? I guess it is a pretty untypical spectator sport anyway and from which one cannot generalize.

The really popular spectator sports appear to be either violent, aggressive or dangerous, like boxing and motor racing. May we assume therefore that any sport which appeals to our baser instincts will be popular, and if so, can we bring back the gladiators please?

Although not usually dangerous, copulation may be both violent and aggressive, so why, I ask, do we not make a public spectacle of sex? There was never a more basic instinct than this! Had there ever been such a spectacle, the laurels, in a gladiatorial sense, would presumably have gone to the most prolific stud rather than the other way round and the theme would have been - fucking, rather than fucked - to death! Or is that being chauvinistic? Which reminds me, the pamphlets say one must not have 'marital relations' for four to six weeks after a heart attack and only then as long as it does not cause pain, or breathlessness. Leaving pain aside, I have never had it off without puffing a bit. It is not like climbing two flights of stairs, you know.

Stan, the man with the pain in his shoulder, who left three days ago, called into the ward during the morning, to collect some paper or other. He came in and had a chat to me and then went across to Edward. I was surprised to hear him decline the invite to exchange telephone numbers with Edward. He explained something about a policy he and his wife had of not pursuing friendships made on holiday and the like. What a silly pair of people and what a miserable attitude! Edward was quite hurt, I could tell.

After the visitors had all left and everyone had been more or less bedded down for the night the Scottish lad, for some reason, felt impelled to talk to me. I cannot remember what he was on about, something to do with how badly he had been treated, but he was telling it to me in such a confidential way. This was a bit odd really, because we were at opposite ends of the ward and the four other patients could not help but overhear. They were all trying to go to sleep anyway and his one-sided conversation must have been very annoying for them. In the end I had to tell him to stop talking as everyone was trying to go to sleep. He really was a bit odd, that lad.

DAY EIGHT

This is the day. The Registrar on his rounds this morning confirmed that I could go home this afternoon. He gave me a date, which is three weeks ahead, when I have to return for a check up. He said that he would review the situation of my ulcer then and that I would probably have a gastroscopy - I believe he called it that - whereby a doctor climbs down my throat holding a mini camera, or something.

Complete rest for the first week and thereafter building up the walking exercise, until by the end of the third week I should be walking a mile.

Edward was positively anti my going home. He told his wife that I had kept him alive. "I don't know what I shall do without you." He was delighted when I told him that Sandra and his wife had exchanged phone numbers. "You must come to tea and we will have it on the lawn."

Sandra arrived for me at about two o'clock and I got dressed in my 'civvies'. Cheryl said "Please say hallo to me when you see me out in New Malden."

The pamphlet did not exaggerate one jot when it spoke of psychological hang-ups about leaving hospital after a heart attack. We reached the ground floor, and the entrance, and I found a chair to sit on, clutching my two large bags of pills, while Sandra went off to get the car. I felt foolishly weak. The ride in the lift had been adventurous enough, but sitting here by myself, waiting for Sandra, was positively petrifying.

I closed my eyes on the ride home, to shut out the traffic and the chaos. I guess one is thrust in upon oneself in a very dramatic way by the experience of a heart attack to an extent that one does not realize until you are confronted by the world again.

It was a beautiful day anyway, sun scorched and happy and the house looked both comfortable and friendly. Sandra had planned it all with great thought. There was a new spreading sunshade on the patio with red and white striped garden chairs beneath it - very festive. She had even popped some bedding plants into the gaps in the borders. When could she have had the time to do it? She spent from morning to night with me in the hospital? Felix the cat came and sat with us.

Sandra had brought one of the leather club chairs down from the living room, into the bedroom, so that I could go from the garden chair to a club chair, in one easy movement.

Perhaps I should describe what a patio house is, to explain the unconventional room relationships. The L-shaped ground floor is arranged around a courtyard, or patio and all the rooms open out into it. The ground floor accommodation comprises the entrance and dining room, off which, into the short front leg of the L, is the kitchen and bathroom in parallel, and beyond which is the principal bedroom. The long leg of the L comprises two further bedrooms and a cloakroom with WC. Upstairs and over the entrance and dining room, is the living room. This opens out, through a conservatory, on to a flat roof over the kitchen, bathroom and bedroom. The house is then repeated by another, which abuts the main bedroom and encloses the patio on its third side.

If you followed all that, take £200 and go straight to MENSA!

The patio design was first developed on the continent, either in Switzerland, or Germany, but certainly during the thirties. Fairacre was the first such development in this country and was designed by Architects Co-Partnership and built in 1964. The principal virtue of the concept is the total privacy it achieves. All of the accommodation at ground floor is lit from windows which open into the patio and that in turn is only overlooked from the flat roof outside the living room at first floor. The plan form is miserly in plot density terms and it is low rise, both factors making it highly suitable for urban situations. I do not know why it has not been more widely used in this country. For my present condition it suits perfectly to have everything accessible on the ground floor; an ideal plan for the old man!

My sister Rene, who is twelve years older than I, said to me a couple of years ago, "You must think positively, think of all the good things about growing old - and then let me into the secret." She always said she could not recommend growing old to anyone. But I was not too depressed that first day home; indeed I was mighty thankful to be here.

Peter rang late afternoon to tell me how the degree examinations had gone. I had not forgotten that this was the day, although it had gotten a little overtaken in my mind by other matters. There were three firsts and three fails, much as predicted, I guess.

Michael later brought me a get-well-soon card from the three external examiners, Ken Martin, Cho Padamsee and Trevor Dannatt. They added a disclaimer to the card saying that although it was not their choice they could see a likeness in the facial expression of the kitten on its cover. I didn't understand, but nevertheless appreciated the thought.

I wobbled my way into bed, relishing its sheer physical comfort and slept for eleven unbroken hours.

DAY NINE

It is only nine days since the heart attack - an event which they say need not alter your life in any way.

"You will benefit physically and psychologically from a return to your normal lifestyle as soon as possible." So says the pamphlet. Unfortunately, I shall not be able to follow this sound advice as I am due to retire before my sick leave will be over.

I really did balls things up, as they say. After heading one of the best Schools of Architecture in the UK for the last twenty-three years, I am to retire at the end of this session. I was told by my deputy, Peter Jacob, to keep next Tuesday evening free and I have been aware of some great conspiracy afoot for that date. On the advice of the doctor however, I have had to call off whatever was planned. And judging from the notice in Building Design this week, it was to have been quite a party.

So, far from returning to normal, I return to one of the biggest landmarks in my life since I went off to war in 1941. It is a time for thought, but not yet, perhaps not just yet ...

I have to get a few other things sorted out in my mind first, things like, will I be able to sit in this house alone ever again? The thought of Sandra going off shopping, let alone to work in Highgate, is terrifying. Suppose I start having those pains again? It hit me completely out of the blue last time, why should it not happen again just like that?

They said at the hospital that I must not think in this way. Clever advice, but impossible to follow. Not that Sandra threatens to move out of my sight. She fusses and frets for my comfort, so that I am utterly spoiled.

Although I could have carried on sleeping blissfully I persuaded myself, and Sandra, out of bed by nine o'clock. I am aware of the need to establish some sort of personal regime in the absence of any external factors like having to get to work. My resolve disappeared after that initial effort though and we sat reading the paper and eating a leisurely breakfast until midday.

The thought of a long soak in the tub seduced me into activity. It has been a week since I last had a bath and the gentle licks with a wet flannel sitting on the edge of the hospital bed were hardly a substitute.

It all has to be done rather slowly; just washing my face makes me puff. But lying in the bath and being sponged down by Sandra is sheer hedonistic delight. I can see why the Romans enjoyed it, although I was using Badedas and not milk, and we omitted some of the other features too, of necessity!

Michael called late in the afternoon and we sat in the patio sipping our whiskeys. Sex might not be allowed yet, but thank God, whiskey is! I am aware of the stresses at college this week, the degree and diploma examinations, but I do not ask. I feel safer in not knowing. I do not trust my reactions somehow, should I hear of all the inevitable problems that crop up at this time.

I asked Michael if he would bring my computer home from my office sometime. It occurred to me that this was a marvellous opportunity to come to terms with it. I have had it for a year, but no way could I claim that I know how to use it. It is an Amstrad 1512 and I have a word processor programme called Wordstar. This is where all the computer buffs tut, tut, and shake their heads knowingly. One thing I do know about computing is that no one agrees about anything and, for sure, I will have the wrong computer, the wrong programme and why did I not ask them about it first, anyway? It is almost as bad as trying to break into Hi-Fi the first time. Everyone else is an expert, but only after you have invested a minor fortune in the wrong things.

Instead of feeling guilty every time I sit down for an hour trying to make it perform, as I did in the office, I can now indulge myself up to my eyeballs.

A guilty conscience is an odd thing really, when you stop to think about it. I am naturally lazy and all my life, like Jiminy Cricket, I have had guilty feelings about it. Sometimes this stirs me out of idleness, when I surprise myself - and others. Not always though. Most of the time I can suppress silly things like guilt, but usually this still leaves just a teeny niggle - residual conscience no doubt.

I had begun to wonder recently whether retirement would liberate me from this beastly problem, so that at last I could enjoy my natural laziness? And here I am talking about indulging myself in working with my computer. Is there no escape?

I finish the day, as I did yesterday, by going slowly up the stairs, clutching my bottle of pills, to watch the television for an hour or so.

DAY TEN

The great new discovery of my life is crosswords. I have always been incredibly inept at answering even the simplest versions, and the tricks compilers get up to, if I am ever able to get far enough to identify them, infuriate me rather than entertain. But I discovered the Times Concise crossword yesterday and completed it, the first crossword I have ever finished! I know it is easy, far simpler than the big one in the Times, but I cannot understand the questions on that one, even when I have the answers.

I found myself turning to the crossword this morning, before I had read the headlines on the front page. This is intriguing. Have I undergone some personality metamorphosis, some physiological cut-over, or is it simply the change of life?

It was a good sight to see Michael arrive with my computer. The question is where to put it? Already the dining room is overwhelmed by my drawing board. We decided that the tea trolley was purpose made for it and Michael did a splendid bit of improvised joinery, cutting a piece of heavy ply to make an extended top to take the computer, key board and printer. The manuals, discs and continuous feed paper sit neatly on the shelf below. I only need my swivel chair from the office to make a very efficient unit. We will have to move soon, at this rate, to a bigger house, one with an office attached.

Sandra took the opportunity, with Michael here, to go out and do some shopping, leaving me for the first time. She probably felt the need to escape from this take-over of her dining room too, poor girl. She did not complain – well, not much anyway. She called at the hospital, while she was out, to collect a certificate for me.

Peter called during the joinery work. He said that the Sixth Year Town Launch had gone off successfully yesterday evening. This was an entirely student-conceived and organised event to replace the exhibition the diplomates normally have in town.

The Diploma Show, or exhibition of the work of the diplomates, is an important event for them. Prospective employers tour the School Shows, or those in London anyway, to headhunt for staff. Last year, Ron Green from Sir Hugh Casson's office, nobbled my three top diplomates, before the results were announced even, a feat which pleased him immensely. He was very chuffed with himself for picking in advance the three 'Diplomates with Distinction'.

Peter also said that the Diploma Examinations had started satisfactorily and that the three external examiners, Geoffrey Broadbent, James Dunbar-Naismith and Geoffrey Darke, all sent me their best wishes.

The Director has appointed Peter Acting Head, and the Academic Registrar told him that, as such, he would chair the Course Examinations Committees. Peter applied for the Headship when it was first advertised last April, but no appointment was made at that time. Although some forty people applied, an adequate short list could not be drawn up and the post is to be re-advertised. The Director has in fact cocked it up badly and has created a lot of ill feeling for himself in the School over this.

Three of the four Principal Lecturers applied for the post and it can be said that each of them could have filled it. Each would have brought something different to the role and, in my opinion, all were much stronger than any of the external candidates. The Director informally interviewed them, as well as the strongest of the external applicants. He had an external assessor with him at these interviews. All of this was quite normal and unexceptional, but no one interviewed at that time last May, has heard a word since. As a result there are a lot of disgruntled people about, so the grapevine has it.

I gathered weeks ago that it was to be re-advertised, so why delay announcing this and why delay the re-advertisement? The simple reason is that there is no one in the Polytechnic to do anything about it other than the Director and he has other things on his mind.

As well as Head of Architecture, I was also Dean of the Faculty of Professional Studies and thus responsible for the Schools of Law and Surveying. When the Headship of Law became vacant due to the retirement of Bruce Renton, his successor would never have been appointed had I not initiated the entire process, including holding informal interviews and drawing up the short list. It was only at that stage that the Director came into the picture when he chaired the appointments' panel.

All of this was quite in order and consistent with my role, but in the case of appointing a new Head of Architecture, as Dean I could only take the process so far. This I did by first identifying a group of people who would be able to advise the director in the appointment and arranging for this group to meet one evening in February, over a glass or two. They included Peter Jones, ex-Chief Architect to the GLC, Vice President of the RIBA and ex-student and staff-member of the School; Peter Ahrends, of Ahrends Burton and Koralek, the winners of the National Gallery Extension competition (which Prince Charles sank without trace!) and an ex-external examiner for the School, and finally Jim Armstrong of Architects Co-Partnership and Visiting Professor to the School of Civil Engineering. The group also included Doris White, Head of Surveying and a Governor. A pretty smart group for the purpose I thought.

They met and agreed upon the sort of person who should be appointed. I then produced a job specification and got the advertisements out. Thereafter I could do no more and thereafter not a lot seems to have been done by anyone else either! At this rate Peter Jacob will be Acting Head for at least a couple of terms. Small compensation for him not getting the job the first time round, but some amelioration perhaps.

DAY ELEVEN

The pain starts in my chest this morning. Not a heavy pain, just a hint of that one, enough to scare the daylights out of me. Is it going to get any worse? It is getting worse. I start sweating. They gave me some tablets to take for the pain, Glyceryl Trinitrate, or TNT, the explosive. One can suck two or three of these under the tongue, but if the pain persists, or gets worse, send for the ambulance. The pain can be angina, or the heart complaining, in which case you stop whatever you are doing and rest, when it should go away. But if it does not go away, it could be another heart attack!

I sit back in the club chair and suck a tablet. It is a bit of a cliff-hanger, waiting to see if you are going to die.

The pain recedes. What a sense of liberation. You hardly dare believe it. I suppose I will get used to this, if I live long enough!

I heard Sandra telling someone on the phone later, "At least we now know the tablets work." I took things a wee bit more thoughtfully for the rest of the day.

Michael came at about five o'clock. He said that the diploma examinations had gone OK, three Commendations and only one failure. That sounds more than OK, more like very well indeed.

In the diploma examination, the candidate submits his/her two-year postgraduate portfolio of work which includes the Major Task. This is a design for a building of the

41

student's own choice, on which he/she spends his final two terms. The design is taken to a very complete stage and includes details of its structural, environmental and constructional content. If, for example, the design is for a concert hall, the student has to demonstrate that it will work acoustically, giving the reverberation times which take account of every square inch of material used in its finishes, plus the audience. He/she is then quizzed for about an hour by an external examiner on the various decisions he has made in his design process. If the student has produced a design of outstanding quality, the examiner will recommend that it receives a Commendation and the Diploma is then awarded - With Commendation. So we had three this year, very well indeed!

With the examinations now finished, the celebrations start. The first of these is the Summer Ball. This is organized by the students and each year they try to go one better than the previous year. The venue this time is the Victorian Pump House at Kew, a very architectural setting. They have held it there before and I recall how brilliant the scene was; the bright evening gowns were a kaleidoscope of colour against the earthy red and green of the machines and the lights sparkled like fireworks in the brass. It was a very hot night and the strawberries and cream were just perfect for it.

I was glad Michael said he was not going. It made my missing it a little more bearable.

DAY TWELVE
Sue Blackstock rang this afternoon to ask Sandra if she would like a 'Dennis-sitter' while she goes shopping? Sandra was trying to work out how she would organize things. It is in this situation that the extended family obviously works. Michael

Blackstock, my nephew, is the only relative I have within fifty miles and all of Sandra's relatives are in Bristol, one hundred and twenty miles away. In these modern times though, when everyone in the family works, including mother-in-law, the extended family probably has less value in this sense. It would be a comfort nevertheless, to know that Aunt Flo, or cousin Pat is just around the corner.

We have lots of friends and masses of acquaintances, but at times like these friends tend to feel they should not intrude too closely into what they see as a very personal problem. We were besieged initially, or Sandra was, by endless telephone calls and the house was suddenly full of beautiful flowers. People were very concerned and solicitous and this, in the first few days, was immensely supportive for Sandra. But I believe she did miss the close support an immediately available relative would have given her, or that which a more imaginative, and hence intrusive, friend could have provided.

The weather continues to be excellent, blue skies, cotton-puff clouds and lots of sunshine, so that we were able to sit in the patio when Michael and Sue arrived. Sandra, thus liberated, brrrrrmd off to do the shopping, the first full scale forage possible for two weeks. I felt just slightly anxious to see her go, but more for Mike and Sue, than myself.

Sue answered the doorbell when it rang. It was Carole and she stood looking at me closely from the dining room door. Carole has beautiful grey eyes and they never fail to give me a lift whenever I see her. I was delighted to see her now, the first time since the attack. I was not surprised to see her by herself, for although both of them had visited Sandra while I was in hospital, Graham has a near pathological aversion for illness and news of my heart attack would have grossly upset him. Carole will now be able to tell him that I look as much as I ever looked and that I do not appear to be imminently dead.

While Sue was making us a cup of tea, Carole asked about the barn conversion and whether we were going ahead with it or not? Carole and Graham have followed its progress from the sidelines with interest and lots of encouragement. They even visited the site a few weeks ago, when they were in Devon. I said how we had not given it much thought at this stage and were certainly not taking any major decisions like that for a bit. I have not thought about the future yet - sufficient unto the day and we will think about tomorrow later.

They are getting screwed up currently about their holiday. They plan to cycle and camp in France, but Sarah, their fifteen-year-old daughter, cannot conceive of anything so boring. The joys of teenage children! A hot and tired Sandra joined us from her shopping spree and we all had a chunter about teenage children and the problems therewith.

DAY THIRTEEN

Although I have had the computer at home for three days I have not made serious use of it yet. Today however, I decided to make a start on writing about this episode of my life. It is a most significant time for me apart from my health. One normally only retires once in a lifetime and the event at best is momentous. I planned for mine over a long period of time and with great care, very conscious that the transition from a full and active professional life to one relieved of all the pressures and responsibilities that it entails will be traumatic to say the least. And now those plans have all been scuppered and I have not got a clue what to do next.

I count myself as being immeasurably fortunate in being able to do architecture. It was an ambition I held as a child when I decided to become President of the Royal Institute of British Architects - that is before I became Prime Minister - or flew a Hawker Fury in Egypt. What I did not then realize was that for real job satisfaction you could not beat teaching. I never did become President and, thank God, I never did finish up in politics in spite of a brief flirtation with the local Liberals. I did fly and something faster than a Fury too. But my great privilege has been to teach, and what is more, to teach architecture.

I actually started my professional life in the office of Sir Hugh Casson, or Mister Casson as he then was, in 1950. I saw the job advertised and came down from Leicester for an interview. The partners, who at that time included Patience Clifford, went through my portfolio and told me they would be in touch. I had just reached the foot of the staircase from the office, when Pat Clifford called me back.

"We want you to have the job, you've built one more house than we have." At that stage I had built three.

I have been forever grateful to Hugh Casson, for the experience he gave me over the next four years and for his subsequent help in my own practice and ever since. I learnt more in the time as his assistant than I ever learnt at college.

We were still emerging from the post war utility period and there was not a great deal of building yet getting under way. Timber was rationed and it needed some skill to make the allowance per house stretch far enough. Flat roofs, mandatory in the Modern Movement, were just about all one could manage within the one and a half standards of timber.

Casson's principal work at that time was with exhibitions. We did the Britain Can Make It Exhibition, the British Industries Fair and there was always the odd exhibition stand to be designed. The great thing about exhibition work for a young architect was the highly compressed design

45

experience it gave. You were designing for a few weeks, supervising construction for a few more and then seeing your creation in three dimensions, before it was torn down and forgotten. In real building, out in the wet as it were, the design/build process can take years.

The ace job, of course, was the Festival of Britain and the 1951 South Bank Exhibition. Casson, as coordinating architect, had an office on site, while we back at Old Brompton Road carried on the main practice as well as designing and detailing the Schools Section of the exhibition. It was immensely exciting, every architect of note in the country was involved and we were busy making history.

John Farmer has very recently written about the genesis of Festival Architecture and while I agree completely with his analysis, at the time it seemed we were doing what came naturally and having a ball. Casson's influence was immense, an architect of incomparable taste and design skill he made it all happen with easy good humour, tact and enough diplomacy to make the Foreign Office give up. His Knighthood was richly deserved.

The then Minister of Works asked Hugh what sort of work he would like to have in the office, after it was all over. "Would you like some industrial building?" "Oh God, not one of those Lobb jobs!" Howard Lobb was a very distinguished architect who had built some rather undistinguished factories.

My role in the office developed into that of running the contracts other than exhibition work. I had the Fairlawn contract, refurbishing the large Georgian House in Kent owned by Peter Cazelet, the Queen's racehorse trainer at that time. We demolished the awful Victorian excrescences and restored the original Georgian building, including putting in an outdoor swimming pool. I remember having great difficulty on one

46

occasion in trying to dissuade Mrs Cazelet from painting a newly created bathroom an awful yellow. I told Sir Hugh about this and he wrote her a brief note.

" ... I don't advise this. You would feel as if you were living in a yellow plastic handbag."

My assistant then was a very beautiful South African girl. She had done ballet and was utterly captivating. We spent some very steamy site visits to Fairlawn, doing things which were never mentioned in the RIBA Plan of Work Stages. I completely lost my heart to her. Unfortunately she was married and the affair ended after six hectic weeks - with lots of bangs - and a whimper!

There was a sequel to this episode. Thirty years later I had a telephone call which my secretary put through saying, "Someone called ...." I could not believe it. I just got as far as saying, "Is it ... ?" and that so familiar lilting voice answered, "Yes, it is!"

She was in London en route to Greece and had rung me for old times' sake. She was only here until the weekend and I was to ring her back to arrange a dinner date. I told Sandra and she was very keen to meet her, but I funked it. I never rang. I really wanted to remember Jennifer as she was thirty years ago, a beautiful, slim, elegant blonde with a voice that caressed like cream.

But to return to my retirement plan, the principal point of this had been getting back to do some architecture. Heads of School retire, but Architects go on forever.

DAY FOURTEEN

The start of another week, apparently it is Monday. I have now lost track of which day it is. I got up yesterday at nine o'clock, my new rising time, and Sandra protested that it was Sunday. Sunday, as yet, is no different from any other day, although I am sure I will adjust once I get a new seven-day week routine established.

We seem to have had our summer, for that gorgeous weather of the last two weeks is now replaced by the old familiar gloomy wet. Thank heavens for my computer.

I started writing yesterday about my retirement plans, the principal move in which was to re-establish a small practice. I first started practising on my own account when I left Casson's office, in 1954. I had a couple of private houses and a few extensions and conversions, not much but by doing a bit of teaching as well it was enough to take the plunge.

Sir Hugh wanted me to stay on in the office and offered me an associateship. If it had been a partnership I guess I would have stayed, although by then I was beginning to feel some divergence of design opinion with Neville Conder, the second partner. He approached his design always with some preconception whereas I start from first principles in the true modernist tradition. It was this which really prompted me to move, plus the prospect of starting my own practice, a cherished ambition of every young architect.

My first house was a great success, 'Southerns' for my sister Vi and brother-in-law, Ron Blackstock. It was a long, low, flat roofed bungalow, very modern, very Bauhaus and was eventually widely illustrated, in D'Aujourdhui, Abitare, as well as in House and Garden, Homes, and The Architects' Journal. The House and Garden write-up brought in further work and gave me the opportunity to experiment with another house at Mereworth, in Kent. My client was an architect's dream, very enthusiastic about my work and seeing himself as my patron put on this earth to enable me to achieve my creative genius. I hope I did not let him down too badly.

It was the first house to be built in the UK using a steel frame which I infilled with cedar-clad panels. It too was widely illustrated. The journalist who wrote it up in the Homes Magazine included another steel framed example, which was a much more elegant piece of design. Her name was Jose Manser, the wife of Michael Manser, who became President of the RIBA a couple of years ago and who of course had designed the other steel framed house! Although this all happened in the late fifties, Michael recalled the episode when he visited the School quite recently.

The first house, 'Southerns', pioneered the notion of underfloor heating and it was the first time this form of heating had been used in the UK - that is since the Romans introduced it two thousand years ago. The heating installation was designed by a heating engineer called Henry Mitchell, a marvellous character who flew an old Harvard trainer up and down the Yangtze River during the war to conceal the noise Wingate was making with his troop movements. Henry used to teach at the Architectural Association where he had a very impressive reputation.

I started doing some teaching for Eric Brown, at the School of Architecture at Kingston College of Art. I found that three days in the office and two at college was an ideal balance, certainly a happy one as far as the bank manager was concerned. The students kept one mentally on one's toes and they appreciated the practical experience one brought to the teaching. In 1964 however, I succumbed to the offer that the Principal, Reginald Brill, made of a Lectureship. He promised that I need not put in any more time than I was then doing, but that I could enjoy the security and pay of a full time post. It was an offer no one could refuse. But within two years I found myself Head of School and with the delicate balance between teaching and practice smashed forever.

I did not concede this at the time and continued the practice, now in partnership with my nephew, Michael Blackstock, who was also an ex-student of mine from Kingston. We finally dissolved the practice and the partnership in the late Seventies when I realized that things were being built which I had never seen on the drawing board.

I became increasingly envious of those of my colleagues who were actively building and now, at the point of retirement from teaching, I looked forward to doing some more architecture.

Today, of course, is the opening of the Degree and Diploma shows. In the past I have usually invited some well known architect to come in and say a few words by way of an opening ceremony, people like Edward Cullinan, Cedric Price, Richard Rogers and so on. We invite lots of would-be employers and friends of the school to join us and it is an enjoyable but fairly low-key event. This year, as it was to have been the last one I would officiate at, everyone said I could pick the principal speaker. I opted for Joanna Lumley! I dictated a letter to her the day before I had my heart attack but in fact it was never sent. I am sure she would have done this for us, but now I will never know. In her place Peter did very well in getting Liz Esteve Cole. I am very sad I cannot be there.

DAY FIFTEEN

I had pains in my chest again this morning, the second time since I have been back from hospital. It is a black moment when it happens, time stands still as if the universe is holding its breath. I'm certainly holding mine, until the TNT takes effect and the pain begins to recede.

As well as re-establishing a practice, a second feature of my retirement plan was to quit London and to get as far away from Kingston as possible. The last thing I want is to meet ex-colleagues in the high street every time I go shopping and have to spiel about how marvellous retirement is. In any case I have lived in London all my life, apart from the war period and four years thereafter while I was at college and I am sick of London. It is incredibly scruffy, ugly and brutish. Londoners also are indescribably ill mannered, boorish and forgettable. I remember on my first post-war trip into France, shortly after the war, how I felt rather similarly about Paris and the Parisians and how pleasant it was to return to civilized England and our trim and tidy countryside. Today, everything is completely reversed - France is spick and span, while this country is like a dustbin.

The utterly selfish behaviour of most Londoners, scattering their litter indiscriminately, parking their cars with total disregard for anyone else in the world, barging along pavements and forcing the elderly, like me, into the gutter without heed, is unparalleled and I can hardly wait to escape.

These two features of my retirement plan, of restarting a practice and of quitting London, came together when we found Boss Hill, a superb piece of land, with a derelict barn on it, in Devon. It consists of four acres of grazing land, sweeping gently down towards the Axe Valley, with marvellous views of the bird sanctuary and the villages of Colyton and Colyford on the other side. The barn stands at the highest part of the land and one can just see the sea between the hills to the south. It is four miles from Axminster and three miles to Seaton, the perfect location as far as we are concerned. The first time we

51

went on to the land and looked down to Colyton and Colyford, I felt I could be happy here.

This was last Easter. We spent a few weeks haggling over the price and finally agreed a figure which was more than we can afford, but sixteen and a half thousand pounds less than he was initially asking! The solicitors are now doing the conveyancing. Immediately after my heart attack Sandra rang our solicitor to tell him to go slow, that is until we know what is happening. I am to see my GP on Friday and a lot will depend upon what he says. I do not want to think about it yet.

    We were in Devon a couple of weeks before my attack, when I took some levels of the site and we met the planning officer. While these people are no longer allowed to make aesthetic judgements on planning proposals, they still exert an all-powerful influence with their planning committees. It is wise therefore to make friends with one's planning officer. He was very helpful and we got along very well, but I detected design prejudices which could be troublesome. He believes that all country cottages should have horizontal glazing bars in their windows! God preserve us from planning officers - and other design-bereft individuals with similar prejudices.

Peter called in late in the afternoon and was followed shortly afterwards by Michael, who had his two sons with him, Tom and James. The two lads are setting off next week to drive around Europe. They start in Holland and then through Germany to Austria and Italy, finally planning to meet up with Jonathan in Milan. It all sounds utterly casual and quite unplanned, like a trip down the high street - "and let's meet for coffee sometime." I would want itineraries, timetables, to say nothing of contingency plans - plural! But perhaps that is why I have the heart attack?

Peter left to go back to college, to check that no one turns up for my retirement party. I realize now just how wise it was to defer this a couple of weeks ago. I do not yet feel strong enough to cope with such an emotional event as that.

DAY SIXTEEN

Today, for the first time, I have walked outside the house. Not very far, but still an achievement. According to Dr Gunraj, I have to walk a mile by the end of the month, that is in a couple of weeks' time.

The design I have produced for the conversion of the barn seems to fit our ambitions beautifully. It is in three bays with the centre bay taken up by an entrance/dining hall and an extravagant galleried staircase, all very baronial and Baillie Scott. The entire west side of the barn is to be glazed, with a balcony at first floor running the whole length of the building. The materials will be stone and timber, both inside and out, natural finishes only with nothing to be plastered or painted. The low-pitched tiled roof will extend out over the west-facing balcony to provide protection to the glazed doors of the bedrooms. There will be two large, stone, open fireplaces, one in the living room and one in the hall, to burn logs which seem to be plentiful.

Perhaps I should take up writing drivel for estate agents!

I have made a model of the building to quarter inch scale, showing the details of the kitchen and bathroom fittings, which everyone can understand more easily than the drawings.

Talking of barns reminds me of Dame Sybil Thorndyke's comment on being told about an old friend of hers who was moving house. "Where are they going?" she asked. "Barnes" replied her daughter. "Poor things, can't they afford a house?"

Sandra bought a book recently, The Challenge of Smallholding; this was after I came home one day saying that sheep were the answer. Four sheep will keep an acre of grass clipped almost like a bowling green and they say that sheep become quite domesticated, if you let them into the house... I don't think Felix would go for that though, or Sandra.

It is a most pleasant thought, four acres of space and freedom, with fresh vegetables, fruit, fresh air and no noise - well - apart from the odd sheep bleating perhaps.

Sandra took the car and collected a new portable colour television from Boots, this afternoon. We needed it to replace our old black and white one in the dining room, which ceased to function unless you gave it a God-Almighty thump. It was when you had to thump it every ten minutes, or so, to keep it going that we thought we ought to replace it. Boots, by way of a sales pitch, gave us a jolly little Walkman, the mini-radio and earphones you see suicides cycling around with in search of an accident. Jonathan, as soon as he saw it said, "I'll take that on holiday with me." It is his twenty-second birthday the day after tomorrow, so guess what we could give him?

Jonathan spent a gap-year after St. Paul's, before going up to Imperial College to read Geology. He came down with a lower second at the same time that the bottom fell out of the oil industry. Not one of his fellow graduates got a job in Geology. Jonathan spent the best part of a year driving a delivery van around, the most highly qualified truck driver in London, before getting a temporary technicians post with BP where he was an over-qualified errand boy. He resigned last week in screaming boredom.

He had to initiate his successor into the duties of the post before he left, another honours Geology graduate from Imperial College! It seems quite immoral to me as an educationalist that enrolment should be permitted into courses which have no job prospects whatsoever. Education must be freely available to everyone capable of pursuing it, and freedom of choice in education is something I would defend to the death. But, when an industry falls flat on its face and it is apparent to everyone that the job market in that industry has completely dried up, then advice should be readily forthcoming to aspiring students.

Neither Jonathan, nor any of his colleagues were given any such advice and I consider this to have been grossly immoral of Imperial College. I am acutely aware of the effect of market forces, of supply and demand reactions and the way in which such forces naturally control the levels of entry to most industries and professions. There is normally little need to intervene into these apparently natural processes, although unforeseen and exceptional trends such as the worldwide collapse of an industry cannot be left to time-sensitive reactions alone and intervention by way of manpower management becomes essential. The DES, through their entry systems of UCCA and PCAS, should have intervened long ago.

The DES has shown quite recently, if misguidedly in the example, that it has the ability to intervene in this way as it did a couple of years ago with Architecture. In what is now seen as a scandalous misjudgement the RIBA invited DES, through its National Advisory Body, to review the provision of architectural education. This would have been in itself an outrageously alien thing for a professional body to do, as was shown by the amazement expressed informally by other bodies such as the Royal Institution of Chartered Surveyors, but to make the invitation in the context of reducing the provision was little short of idiocy.

However idiotic, the DES rapturously welcomed the invitation. At a time when the government was obsessively

55

following a policy of reducing the provision of all higher education, to be asked by a professional body to come in and do that to its educational system was manna from heaven and particularly when that system happened to be a very expensive one with its unique five year mandatory student grant.

So, the review duly happened and on the evidence made available, the reviewing body, the Esher Group, recommended a reduction of provision by a colossal 30%. This recommendation was accepted and implemented and two Schools of Architecture were duly closed. The rest were given appropriately reduced intake quotas. That was two years ago. Now, two years later, the President of the RIBA is saying what a terrible mistake it all was - admittedly a different President - and that the profession is now short of qualified architects! Unfortunately, of course, the DES has already made the cuts and I cannot see them now giving away the massive saving they have made in student grants without a lot of argument, if ever.

Meanwhile, and in accordance with an EEC Directive, an architect from any EEC country can now come in to the UK and practice. The President of the RIBA is therefore justified in being worried as he can now see all those new inner-city rebuilding contracts going to continental architects. So much for the selfish protectionism displayed by the previous councillors who voted for a policy to intervene in the natural process of supply and demand.

This is not being wise after the event, for the Standing Conference of Heads of Schools of Architecture used every means available to it, at the time, to persuade Council of its folly. The persistence of the RIBA however, to ignore every bit of advice it received resulted in a complete rupture between them and the Schools, even to the point where collectively the Schools were asking the Architects Registration Council of the UK to take back to itself the validation process from the RIBA.

The RIBA appears to have come to its senses however and with the advent of a new President it is anxiously trying to repair the fences.

The latest move in that direction is the quite astonishing appointment of the chairman of the Standing Conference of Heads of Schools of Architecture to chair the Education Committee at the RIBA. They have had to make him a Vice-President as well to do it!

It has been a sad and regrettable episode for the RIBA, where in the past wiser counsel has usually prevailed. I believe that it was the permanent officers who actually failed, rather than the councillors. Presidents and Councils come and go, but the officers are there to provide the institute's memory and, like the civil service, to prevent the worst of any government's excesses. It is no coincidence that Council has recently received the report from a firm employed to investigate the management of the Institute and that as a result heads have already started to roll. The pity is that it has taken so long - it should have happened ten years ago!

DAY SEVENTEEN

In pursuit of my one-mile goal, I walked halfway around the courtyard in front of the house. From such small beginnings ...

John Farmer rang to ask if he could visit and I was delighted to see him when he arrived in the late morning.

The Kingston School of Architecture is renowned for being blessed with one of the best, if not the best, staff teams in any School of Architecture. This can be accounted for by a number of factors, not least that we are a London school and therefore have a massive reservoir of talent to draw upon. But this fact alone makes us no different from the other London schools. A major factor has to be that over the years I have consistently filled a third of my teaching establishment with part-time staff. This is a very high proportion which no other school reaches. Currently there are about twenty practising architects who spend one or two days a week in the studios and most of these are young people with about five years experience.

Many of them, just like myself when I started teaching, are trying to support new practices. They stay with the school on average about three years and then their practices flourish enough to wean them away.

The odd one or two every few years come across as born teachers with something vital to say and these we try not to let escape. Every one of my fourteen full time members of staff I captured from the part time ranks. Not one of them came through the normal channels of advertisement, interview and appointment. They were all tried in the studios for a few years, proved themselves and then succumbed to the offer of an established Lectureship, thank heavens!

Kingston is also a very comfortable and happy place to work and the campus at Knights Park is unquestionably the happiest in the Polytechnic. It was the original College of Art, dating from 1939, and the present mix of disciplines is the same as that of the original College.

In 1970 the first Director of the Polytechnic did his damndest to destroy the ethos of the Art College in its merger with the College of Technology; mercifully he failed. The original college was a great deal stronger than he was ever conscious of, and so its Schools survived this attempted emasculation. The final Principal of the old College of Art, Wilfred Fairclough, must now feel great satisfaction that the

Schools he nurtured so successfully are all flourishing in spite of this early mismanagement.

The present Director is fortunately of different stock. He is acutely ambitious and therefore keen to use anyone, or anything, that may be of help in his advancement of the Polytechnic. In recognizing the intrinsic quality of the Art and Design Schools, as well as that of the School of Architecture, he is willing to support them materially as vehicles which will carry the Polytechnic forward in the wake of their own progress. This is, of course, good news for the Schools concerned and it makes them good places to work in.

If my staff in architecture are amongst the best teachers in the business, then John Farmer is one of the best teachers amongst my staff. He came to the school with a great deal of practical experience having been responsible for some massive building schemes including hospitals and university building. I employed him at the time for his practical experience in putting large buildings together. He brought with him however, a very powerful intellect and a questioning mind which over the next few years sampled many sources of knowledge. His approach was always fresh and original and he gradually developed a unique set of attitudes which put him slightly apart from everyone else. John became a bit of a loner and certainly a law unto himself, to coin two hackneyed but apt clichés.

I must not overstate this description of John's qualities, nor make him sound too odd because I could say more or less the same thing about everyone else on the staff. They are all highly individualistic in their architectural philosophies, a truly pluralist group of teachers and this has always been one of Kingston's strengths.

John successfully got it together a couple of years ago, and after a year's study leave he was awarded his Doctorate by the Royal College of Art.

We talked about the theme of his thesis this morning, a fascinating theory about the genesis of the new brutalism and the response of English people to war and its effect upon their art and architecture. He has got a publisher for his book which is based upon his doctoral thesis, so look out for it. It will be very readable - he is, after all, an excellent teacher!

According to my diary, I should be at a meeting of the Faculty of the British School at Rome this morning, selecting next year's Rome Scholar in Architecture. This is the most prestigious prize for students of architecture. It enables the winner to spend a year at the British School in Rome studying an approved topic in the ambience of a Lutyens building in the Eternal City. What a fantastic experience for a young architect!

It is Jonathan's birthday tomorrow, which is always a slightly traumatic event. I separated from my first wife in 1972, when Jonathan was seven. He came and lived with me thereafter and his birthdays up to his mid-teens were quite uncomplicated. More recently however, they have posed for him an emotional problem. With whom does he spend his birthday, with Sandra and me, or with Joan, his mother? He solves the dilemma now by escaping off somewhere and this year he is going to Cornwall, to a weekend beach party.

Michael looked in on his way home from college and Sandra's half-sister, Jane arrived as he was leaving. Jane graduated last year from Loughborough, where she read Ecology. She is now working with the magazine called Nature, a reasonable use of her degree it seems. She is a lovely girl, so very sensible and kindly. Jonathan and she get along very well - they seem to be on the same wavelength.

DAY EIGHTEEN

Jonathan was collected this morning by Fiona and another couple of his fellow geology graduates. They motored off to their Cornish beach party, in dismal rain. What else would one expect in mid-July - summer?

I feel that I am making reasonable progress as I walk out to Acacia Grove, all of two hundred yards there and back. I have an appointment to see my GP this afternoon and I do want to report favourably.

Peter called just as we were about to leave to see the doctor. We drove round in the car and I puffed my way into the surgery. God knows what happened then but I felt terrible, very breathless. Thinking about it later I guess I gave myself an attack of the anxieties. I could hardly talk to Dr Sherski and he must have had a pretty poor impression of my condition. After sounding me over he proceeded to issue lots of do's and don'ts, well mostly don'ts - in fact all don'ts!

He said he did not advise going ahead with converting the barn, nor indeed moving to anywhere in the country which is a bit isolated.

"You must be practical about this, choose somewhere which has a good access road and is close to a hospital!"

He did modify that last one, perhaps thinking he was being a bit too practical for morale.

"Well, somewhere close to a doctor I mean."

Sandra asked, a little desperately perhaps, trying to salvage something from his pessimism, "What about a holiday, doctor, we thought of a couple of weeks in Brittany?" He shook his head - firmly.

"No, I don't want him to leave the country just yet. You cannot get back in a hurry should you need to. He certainly mustn't fly." He thought for a few moments and then relenting, "Perhaps a local holiday by the sea, somewhere nice and flat."

And that was it. Driving back to the house I said to Sandra, "I am not fucking dead yet!"

But it was all very depressing. I know what the situation is, I am not daft, but one needs encouragement at this time, not gloom and doom.

Michael came at half past six, bless him, and had the brunt of our depression. He brought with him a large paper mock-up of a tombstone. It was inscribed 'In affectionate memory of the Faculty of Professional Studies hereby laid to rest.'

They had had a very liquid lunch today apparently, to bury the Faculty. Everyone had signed the thing and then they had decided to send it out to me with a bottle retrieved from the wake. Someone had written on it "This is in extremely poor taste!"

Then again, after dinner, we had more visitors, Carole and Graham. Graham, presumably, had at last screwed up his courage to visit the dead and dying. He looked at me closely and was obviously surprised to see me looking so well. He said so. I was delighted to see him. Graham is a rabid, fanatical socialist and we have spent many happy hours disagreeing with each other, mortally. I would miss my arguments greatly with Graham. Aside from politics, he has a wicked sense of humour.

It was a happy chance that they visited on this night.

DAY NINETEEN

I skipped my bath today, I felt too pooped and too depressed to bother. I took the drawing of the barn conversion off my drawing board and rolled it up.

While I have to agree with the doctor that I could not cope with the hassle of getting it built at this stage, I did hope that it would be possible some time not too far ahead. Not only was it going to fulfil a big ambition, to build my own house, but it was also designed to fill that first year of retirement.

So, what now?

DAY TWENTY

Although today is Sunday, it is the same as any other day. It is even raining, just like any other day.

Sandra says she would like to see me take Sundays off. Off what? Off this hectic round of fuck all, I guess. I wished I were doing something from which I could 'take off'.

I guess I am not inherently lazy, as I have always thought. My conscience has never allowed me to be and it is too late in the day now to learn. I certainly cannot settle for being an invalid forever. It is too boring. Think positive, that's it, think constructively, and all that garbage - as if one can switch on and off like the cooker.

Whatever else happens, I would still like to move away from London. In thinking about an urban situation, as distinct from Boss Hill, we talked about Sidmouth as a possibility. It is a very orderly, kempt sort of place and favourite for retired ladies and gentlemen. Now Dr Sherski would surely approve of Sidmouth? However, I don't!

So we move on round the coast, using our, by now, very well thumbed map of the UK. We next come to Torbay. Torquay and Paignton are out, for obvious reasons, but Brixham and west of Brixham give us pause. I recall Brixham Harbour favourably and the countryside thereabouts is very pleasant too. Perhaps we should take another look at that area and we resolve to do this, just as soon as I can travel.

To say this is a funny period would be the understatement of the year. Since the attack I have been living in a detached world insulated from reality. No, not from reality, because nothing could be more real than the world I now occupy. It is the previous world which is now unreal, like a dream populated with dream-like characters and the present reality is far simpler than that previous one. I live in a timeless bubble and now and then people from elsewhere pop in momentarily, and pleasantly, but without actually making contact, like familiar film characters who never step down from the screen.

I could convince myself that this is a much more comfortable world I suppose, more predictable and controllable, but who am I fooling?

DAY TWENTYONE

Each day now I try to walk a wee bit further and today I got out of the estate and walked halfway up Acacia Grove - very slowly and very conscious of a frailty I must not tempt.

We got on to the topic of moving and then we started questioning the logic of moving to Devon. We originally settled upon Devon because a) it is a nice place, b) it is closer to Brittany and Normandy than most other places, c) one can sail in Devon and d) it is cheaper than the Home Counties.

We did consider Norfolk at one point, but abandoned the idea because it did not meet the requirement b). Now, and on re-analysis, this bit of reasoning failed to stand up, as we are not likely to be going to France all that frequently. The logic of the original thinking was similar to that which I have always used in buying my motorcars where criterion number one has been their ability to cruise effortlessly on motorways - and then I spend fifty weeks of the year driving around town!

Norfolk too is a nice place, one can even sail there and it is certainly cheaper than London! Norwich must be one of the loveliest cities in the country, very drawable, with super shopping and they have managed, more or less, to keep the car out.

Michael came, while Sandra was out shopping, the boot of his car bulging with the big swivel chair from my office. I recall saying something about only needing my office chair to complete my computer unit in the dining room!

There is a meeting this evening of Fairacre Management Ltd., the management company of the estate on which we live. Now this is a real microcosm of power politics where everything goes, including intrigue, slander, blackmail and even nepotism. Being a registered company, we have a board of directors, a company secretary and, of course, a chairman. There are only fourteen freehold houses on the estate and ten leasehold flats and the owners are the company shareholders, but it could be a mighty industrial corporation the way some of them behave.

I agreed to become chairman out of self-preservation and not for self-aggrandisement, not that you would notice much opportunity for that. I merely wished to protect my investment from the weird and bizarre machinations of some of my odder neighbours. The development is unique and now forms a mature estate with attractive landscaping, typifying modern architecture of the sixties at its best. Strong covenants in the freeholds and leases are designed to protect the overall appearance of the scheme and no alterations are permitted to the externals of the properties. So we have owners removing their front doors and replacing them with totally inappropriate mock Georgian panelled versions, complete with leaded light and bottle glass lanterns. If that is their taste why the hell buy a protected modern house in the first place? Another man wants to chop down all the trees within feet of his house and emerges at night with wicked secateurs to prune anything growing nearby. Yet another house owner wants to build barbecues and trellis arbours, of ye-olde cottage vintage, everywhere. Taste is a very personal thing, that is until it becomes a community issue, when it has to conform to the community standard. There is no end to this argument I know, but I retreat behind the covenants, which everyone knew about when they bought their houses. If they felt they would be unable to abide by them, they had no business moving in. I rest my case.

Another issue connected with this management process is a question of style. This is a community and in the past it has operated in a very friendly and neighbourly fashion. We do rely upon goodwill to achieve any corporate objective. I, for one, do not take kindly to being pushed around by neighbours. You know how it can be sometimes when someone gets a little authority and they start behaving like a mini-Hitler — well, it happened here. A couple of honorary officers, who were otherwise quite normal people, started throwing their collective weight around a bit too heavily. For example, near-abusive and certainly very insensitive notes were sent out about late payment of maintenance charges.

"You are one of the last to pay. If you are hard up come and tell me about it." Why the hell should anyone have to report on one's financial status to a neighbour?

The chairman, when he remonstrated with them about taking independent action, was told, "I'm only prepared to do this job as long as I do it my way and without asking anyone else about it." They then made the mistake of resigning and the chairman, being a much wiser person, accepted their resignations with much relief.

Please do not think I am denigrating all of my neighbours, because with the exception of only one or two out of a population of about sixty, they are all charming, kindly and thoroughly desirable people.

The honorary secretary, who called the meeting this evening to talk about various work that needs to be done around the estate, is very thoughtfully insulating me, as current chairman, from any aggro. And I gather from Sandra, who went to the meeting, that there was indeed some deliberate stirring going on, but only from one source. Meanwhile, Jon and I had a pleasant evening watching the tele.

DAY TWENTYTWO
Sandra is a school registrar, or more specifically, the senior administrator of a girl's independent day school at Highgate. She is an excellent administrator which I can state from first hand experience as she was my Faculty Administrative Officer some fifteen years ago and before that, for a spell, Acting Academic Registrar.

It is now three weeks since she has been to work and while everyone at Channing has been very sympathetic and kind, with large bunches of flowers from the head and the staff and messages of support generally for us both, Sandra is concerned, I can tell. She has arranged to go up to Highgate this afternoon to see the deputy head and Michael is coming in to 'Dennis-sit'.

Michael is the Director of Computing in the school and this should give me the chance to have a bit of dual on my word processor.

DAY TWENTYTHREE

I walked up to the end of Acacia Grove today, which must be about a quarter of a mile, there and back. Peter Jacob arrived as we were walking home and I had to decline his offer of a lift, in the interests of the exercise.

DAY TWENTYFOUR

The fourth Test has started and Gatting put Pakistan in to bat, a mistake apparently, because the wicket is playing beautifully and they scored smoothly all day long.

British Telecom arrived to install our new telephones, one of which is a cordless radiophone you can wander around the house with. The engineer used the television power socket though and this deprived me of half an hour of Test Match.

It was very pleasant to see Michael Shoul this afternoon. He is one of the four Principal Lecturers in the school and a man of great intellect and integrity. The students either worship him, or hate him, the latter because he demands more of them than they are capable of giving. He led the team which put together the recently validated Masters Course in Architectural Design. This was of significance as it is the first Masters in Architectural Design to be offered by any Polytechnic or University School of Architecture in the United Kingdom.

Design is a controversial topic and one which has generated an enormous amount of debate and argument over the years. At the Clapham Omnibus level, and that is the level I put Prince Charles along with all the other lay commentators, there is total disagreement about good and bad design, disagreement usually misinformed by prejudice and dogma. At the designer, or expert (?) level, there is total disagreement about good and bad design, informed by education/training - and prejudice and dogma! So what hope has the layperson in making sense of the problem?

By design, incidentally, I mean the process of creating something which has an original quality and in which others can identify beauty, appropriateness and all sorts of other meritorious qualities. One can see that trying to define the word even presents problems, let alone attempting to define the process.

I have been trying to teach design for thirty years, but I am less confident now in the exercise than I was thirty years ago - when I thought I knew all about it. In fact, no one can teach the subject of course, although many think they can and indeed do try. All one can do is to provide the student with the opportunity to practise at designing and then by criticism develop his design judgement.

DAY TWENTYFIVE

I walked to the surgery this morning, to collect a prescription, a distance of about half a mile. I felt quite fit and happily started out later for another walk, getting as far as the end of Acacia Grove. Then I remembered I had left my pills behind!

We have decided to forget Devon as a result of our latest analysis and to switch to Norfolk. Sandra rang about a hundred estate agents and asked for details of properties around Norwich and up to the coast. I am very sad about abandoning Boss Hill, but the hassle of just moving house will probably be bad enough, let alone having to build it first.

Pakistan carried on scoring smoothly all day, putting on 40 or so runs. The wicket is doing nothing, so it looks like a draw, how dull!

DAY TWENTYSIX

Another first, I went shopping this morning, around the corner out of Acacia Grove, to the baker's and the deli, and again, a bit later, along the High Street to the camera shop - about two-thirds of a mile. On the way back, we stopped to talk to Graham who was out cleaning his car. Is this the beginning of a new order of social intercourse, I ask myself?

England batted carefully - no, ponderously, all day.

DAY TWENTYSEVEN

Just to make life that tiny bit more difficult, I have an allergy reaction to house dust, amongst other things. Today I stupidly wore an old cardigan which had obviously gathered dust over the years hanging in a cupboard. The result of being unable to breath through a blocked nose gets completely out of proportion in its effect. One wakes up at night feeling as if one's throat is lined with sandpaper and unable to moisten one's lips with a tongue converted to buckram.

The sunshine tempted us to drive to Homebase to buy some potting compost for the new tomato plants. I left thirty plants in the greenhouse, grown from seed, when I went into hospital and they were one of the minor casualties of the event. Sandra bought four replacement plants the other day. Why does one bother to grow tomatoes each year, I wonder? They are cheap enough to buy, an awful chore to grow and I'm not all that fond of tomatoes anyway.

Coming back to this question of design, one aspect which people get bogged down with concerns fashion. Fashion does influence design and this is most evident in the world of dress design, where fashion can change overnight and what was exciting one day is boring the next. To a lesser extent fashion is also very influential in automotive design, to a lesser extent that is in that the time span for fashionable attrition is in months rather than weeks. In other words one can say that fashion becomes less and less relevant the more permanent in nature the object becomes. If this is so it follows that architecture should be relatively free from the influences of fashion. Indeed, Sir Christopher Wren wrote, "Architecture aims at eternity and therefore is the only thing incapable of modes and fashions in its principles."

One could argue of course that architecture no longer aims at eternity and I would happily settle for the odd half-century. However long it should last though, a building does involve a massive investment these days and it surely is not much sense to build for brevity.

Unfortunately we, the consumers of design in whatever form, are more and more manipulated by the providers. It is good for business to build obsolescence into the product, so that Joe Public is impelled to buy new to stay 'with it' and the fashion and motorcar industries have grown fat and influential over the years on this ploy.

It all started in 1907 with the formation of an organisation in Munich known as the Deutscher Werkbund. This was an association of artists, designers, architects and manufacturers who got together to develop styling in relation to economy and mass production. It is now commonplace in all product design fields and we, the suckers, go out and buy our new cookers, refrigerators, vacuum cleaners, cameras and other consumables, long before the old ones are worn out, just to keep up with the Joneses. A less than agreeable outcome of the Modern Movement!

Happily, this tendency did not bother architecture and it remained aloof from the influences of the salesman and the advertising agent until relatively recently. Built in obsolescence could hardly be developed in a field which practised revivalism and where consumers actually demand buildings in neo-this and neo-the other.

However, even architecture was vulnerable and in the event, succumbed. Fashion was finally introduced, not by the salesman, but by a modern excrescence on the profession called the architectural journalist, a creature without the commercial value even of the salesman. Indeed the architectural journalist, aj for short, is a creature without use, or value, to anyone other than himself. He does not serve the public who does not read him in the professional press and who would not understand a word he wrote even if they tried. He certainly does not serve the profession, some of whom cannot understand what he writes either. He is read avidly however, by teachers of architecture, the lesser of whom then reuse what he has written, in the absence of anything of their own to say.

Unfortunately, the aj is also read most avidly by the sponge-like student and it is here that he does the greatest damage.

The successful aj is the one who discovers the most offbeat, weirdo architecture. Anything goes, as long as it is new, vaguely shocking and preferably outrageous. Stores and offices have been built in the States, where the elevational brickwork has been so constructed as to appear to be peeling off the front of the building. There is an actual design philosophy which supports this extraordinary approach and intellectually it is stunning. But the users of the building who are not aware of these mental games can only gawp and say "what the hell?"

Quite recently, I was assessing some drawings produced by a diploma student, the technical drawings of an office building he had designed and they were extremely accomplished. However, the design involved a great peeling sheet of elevation, just like the American example. This was misguided plagiarism and where the originators probably knew what they were doing, this student was merely copying a fashion. Had the journalists not written in such excited terms about the original, and had his tutor been more questioning about design justification, perhaps the student would have made his own judgement - a much more desirable process.

These journalists 'discovered' the apparent virtues of stage set architecture, and design based upon children's building blocks, and as a result of the publicity they gave it, we are now suffering from a surfeit of segmental arches, pyramidal arches, and all the other crude geometric building block shapes, in every other housing scheme built. One notable architect has achieved national status with his nursery-derived design, which I predict will become as unfashionable as suddenly it became modish. Unfortunately, we will have to continue living with his eminently datable Mickey Mouse buildings, long after he has passed on, and all because a journalist, who cannot be held accountable, 'discovered' this 'new' architecture, sold a book or two and thus created a fashion.

Post-Modern architecture is said by one of these illustrious writers, to have developed a richer language of architecture based on metaphor, historical imagery and wit.

Another way to put this I suggest, would be to say it is an architecture without substance, like stage set design, good for an evening but a yawn thereafter.

It is remarkable how wit has suddenly become an important ingredient in architecture and when identified by these journalists, loudly applauded. How sad that Palladio, Frank Lloyd Wright, Aalto, et al., all overlooked it in their time. According to my Oxford dictionary, wit concerns 'the utterance of brilliant or sparkling things in an amusing way ... That quality of speech or writing ... calculated to surprise and delight by its unexpectedness.' Wit, in other words, demands spontaneity and not even Oscar Wilde would get away with saying something endlessly, no matter how witty it was.

How on earth a piece of architecture can assume a witticism is beyond my comprehension and yet it is commonplace for writers today to invoke this literary allusion. It is so thoughtless and demonstrates the awful effect of fashionable writing upon empty minds and is reminiscent of the story about the Emperor's new clothes. There are enough immutable truths and fundamental principles in architectural design to do battle with without having to introduce bogus irrelevancies like fashion and wit. I would shoot all architectural journalists, or at least ban them from schools of architecture.

DAY TWENTYEIGHT

Lots of houses from Norfolk estate agents this morning, about fifty percent of which are worth looking at too. We were relieved to find that prices have not yet become unreasonable, as we feared they might well have done since the electrification of the railway line to Norwich. The next problem is getting up there to see them. So we went for a walk around the block to consider the matter.

The Test Match is absorbing, with England putting on 500-odd and Gatting a century, a Boy's Own captain's innings.

DAY TWENTYNINE

I had a miserable night again, with a completely bunged up nose. It really is a condition which produces effects out of all proportion to the cause. And the trouble with all the patent nasal sprays is that they seem to make things worse after their effects have worn off. Surely someone could produce a spray which did not do this?

I wrote the other day about fashion in design and in the process exposed a prejudice or two, which makes me feel slightly uncomfortable. Thinking about this I began to question why that should bother me? Prejudices are generally assumed to be undesirable in that they close the mind to what might otherwise be enlightening. In pre-judging something one may well miss its point entirely and one therefore bends a lot of effort in trying to keep an open mind. One of the principal effects of education is, after all, to promote an open mind.

However, no one ever designed a thing of merit without knowing it was right. Designers are arrogant - they have to be. They have to know that what they are doing cannot be done better by anyone else, otherwise they would have to give up. Designers will suffer agonies in the creative process, agonies of frustration and uncertainty, but once conception has happened and the design is started, they then have to know it is right.

It is normal for a student to display his design and to receive a public criticism on it. A group of tutors sit around the work and pontificate upon its merits and otherwise. This 'crit' process is so standard in design education that every school has its Crit Room. However, I have never seen one student over the thirty years of my experience receive this criticism with an open mind. Most receive it politely, nodding at the more obvious points and only querying the obscure ones. Some however, take the crit as a personal affront, an attack upon their very souls and they openly spurn the advice they are offered. None, I repeat not one, takes the advice with a truly open mind.

I have always contended in the school that end-of-project crits are a complete waste of time, but such is the entrenched status of the ritual I never got them supplanted. Tutors insist upon spending hours pontificating to young, arrogant designers, who have just committed their very souls in a project which they believe, nay, know is right. The teaching occurs in the tutorial, not in the crit! I sometimes think that the tutors are more wrapped up in some sort of ego-trip than they are in edifying their students.

So, I contend that to be prejudiced is arrogant, but as a designer has to be arrogant then perhaps prejudice is not the undesirable quality it is always cracked up to be. I can therefore stop feeling uncomfortable when I display my prejudices.

DAY THIRTY

More houses from Norfolk. We spent the entire morning reading the estate agents' blurb and classifying them into three piles, maybe, no, and why waste our time.

Today I went back to the hospital, to the chest clinic, for a check up. In the event Dr Gunraj was relatively happy. He wants me to have a 24-hour ECG and to follow this with a Barium Meal to check out the ulcer. I had forgotten about that.

DAY THIRTYONE

I walked to the Royal Oak, a distance of one mile there and back. It might not have been exactly a brisk walk, but it was a mile! Inspired by the achievement, I set off again in the afternoon to walk to the bank and the newsagent.

So, I overdid it! I had pains in my chest this evening, sitting quietly watching the tele. Sandra was downstairs doing some typing. I could understand it if they happened when I was running up the stairs, or doing something similar, but when they occur out of the blue like this, it worries me.

DAY THIRTYTWO

I felt a bit groggy today, very tired and apart from a short walk up the road I spent most of the time wrestling the computer, trying to get it to print in Near Letter Quality mode.

DAY THIRTYTHREE

If I could get a decent night breathing as God intended through my nose, I am sure I would feel half as good again.

Today is Saturday, so my diary says. We drove to Cheam to do the weekend shopping. I suppose that one day we might challenge the Saturday shopping ritual and go out on a Friday when the rest of the world is at work!

We did not expect to see Carole and Graham this evening as they are off to France tomorrow, but they arrived nevertheless, soon after nine. Perhaps other people do not agonize over their holiday packing as I do. The very thought of it now makes my stomach lurch.

The topic for our customary argument tonight was society's deplorable dive towards money grabbing and materialism. Graham sees it all as Mrs Thatcher's fault and he is undoubtedly right, but I had to argue that the Victorians were worse, what with the Satanic Mills bit and the Empire and that. Sandra feared the imminence of another heart attack!

DAY THIRTYFOUR

Sandra has really discovered my computer and as soon as I disappear into the bathroom in the morning she gets on to it.

Normally I then claim it back when I emerge, but this morning I went off and pottered. My plants, showing amazing empathy, all seem to be suffering as well. The japonica appears to have died, a very large and hitherto healthy hebe has given up and a few of my favoured azaleas likewise. I have never before had such a casualty rate and I think it shows what a good gardener I was.

My next bit of housekeeping concerned the Napoleon Hat mantelpiece clock. It stopped working a few years ago after it was moved. Today I got the spirit level and with the help of paper wedges got it really sorted out. It went for fifteen minutes. Why the hell does it now stop after fifteen minutes each time? What on earth in its clockwork innards causes it to tick away for just so long - and then stop? How does it time itself to keep such good timing to be irregular? I am a patient, reasonable person, but this sort of mechanical obtuseness makes me feel like smashing it.

I complain bitterly to Sandra for hogging my computer and shame her out of my seat.

DAY THIRTYFIVE

Sandra went over to Channing today, to do the best part of a day's work, the first time she has been back for thirty-five days!

I had a telephone call from an ex-student, Martin Branston, who distinguished himself, and the school, by winning the Rome Scholarship in 1966. He was my first success on becoming head of school. I was sad to have to take a rain check on his lunch invitation.

It was in 1966 that I established the Architectural Psychology Research Unit in the school - real innovatory stuff. At that time the social sciences were still respectable disciplines although they do come in for a bit of stick these days, especially sociology!

There was virtually no pure research going on in schools of architecture at that time and very little applied research either. Whatever was happening would have been in connection with industrialised building and materials performance, although there was little enough of that judging from the building failures of the seventies. We began searching for a worthwhile topic and I had a conversation with an acquaintance who was a clinical psychologist at Barming Institute. We started talking about how people reacted to the environment and Alan Dabbs had lots to say about perception, response to colour and so on, all of which seemed to have a great relevance for the architect.

So, I invited him to give a series of lectures to the final year of the Diploma Course with a title something like - The Human Condition in the Environment - or words to that effect. They were very successful and I persuaded Alan to take a part-time contract and to spend at least a day a week with us. I did want to develop this theme which appeared to have a lot of mileage in it. I later took one of my senior tutors, a South African called Basil Honikman, with me up to the RIBA where we sounded them out on the possibility of a research topic around architecture and the social sciences.

The man we spoke with in the education department, Bill Hillier, thought it sounded a valid notion and gave us a lot of encouragement. Hillier, incidentally, is now a senior tutor at the Bartlett School of Architecture, London University, doing something in what he calls architectural morphology.

My next move was to persuade my boss, the Principal of the Art College, Wilfred Fairclough, to give me the finance for a couple of research assistants. For the second time in our relationship, Wilfred demonstrated his faith in me by saying yes, the first being when he appointed me Head. So the research unit was formed and I appointed a sociologist, a social anthropologist and, I believe, an economist, a very odd mix indeed. It was obviously necessary that they should be directed by an architect and I asked Basil Honikman to do this.

The unit spent the first year writing its own programme virtually and there was a great deal of talk and argument as each of the disciplines tried to understand and accommodate the others. I soon switched the economist for a psychologist and thereafter the others were replaced also by psychologists.

The first theme to emerge concerned the way people perceived the environment and in attempting to classify this the unit began to use a methodology called factor analysis. Basil Honikman went on to produce a doctoral thesis on this theme, only being beaten in a matter of weeks by David Cantor at Strathclyde for the first PhD in what is now known as Environmental Psychology. Professor David Cantor has subsequently gone on to earn himself a reputation in helping the police to catch psychopathic killers and Basil to a chair of architecture in the States.

I had developed this field of research from a natural interest, marrying architecture and my second passion psychology to presage in this country what has now become, in the words of Liam Hudson, a major industry of Environmental Psychology. I did not then know that the marriage of architecture and the social sciences had also been arranged in Utah a year or so previously. So, it was a good idea and one which was bound to crop up somewhere sooner or later.

Today, the Kingston Architectural Psychology Research Unit publishes the international 'Architectural Psychology News Letter' on its own behalf and jointly with the international organization known as IAPS.

The Editor is Susan-Ann Lee, a psychologist who has been on the school staff since 1969 and who is now one of the towers of strength in the field. Amongst her numerous other duties she lectures the area of subjects we now call Man/Environment Studies, which are no longer confined to architecture, but extend into things like Computing - a marvellous vindication, if one is required, of the original notions developed with Alan Dabbs some twenty-odd years ago.

DAY THIRTYSIX

I went along to the hospital this morning to be wired up for the twenty-four hour ECG. I emerged with numerous wires stuck to my chest, beneath my shirt and trailing out to a small black box on my belt. They said that unfortunately I would not be able to receive the Test Match commentaries with it.

81

Jonathan goes away tomorrow and he was very busy all day preparing and shopping. He is getting understandably excited about it - two months touring around Europe, from Norway down to northern Spain and then southern Spain, back up to the south of France and finally to Milan.

Michael called and stayed, poor chap, for three hours, wrestling my computer to get Near Letter Quality on the printer, just as I had done the other day. No way does the software switch it on as it should.

DAY THIRTYSEVEN

I went back to hospital this morning to be unplugged. In just the same way that one's tooth stops aching the moment you step into the dentist's waiting room, my heart never missed a beat the whole time I was wired up to the 24 hour ECG.

Jonathan was finishing his packing by the time we got back and I was no longer able to ignore the fact that he is going away for a couple of months. I know that I will feel stupidly emotional about it when the time comes and I am glad that Tim is going with him to the station.

He left at two o'clock and is catching the five fifty ferry from Dover to Ostend, arriving at Stavanger on Friday morning, some thirty-six hours later. He went off with an enormous backpack. God, what a thing it is to be young and fit.

By way of distraction we drove down to Surbiton, shopped at Sainsburys, had a haircut and a new battery fitted in my Seiko.

DAY THIRTYEIGHT

I woke halfway through the night with angina pain and it took a couple of Trinitrate tablets to ease it. The book says tell your doctor if this happens and I went to see him this morning.

He said we cannot do anything until we have the results of the ECG, which should be next week, but that I should ask the hospital then about seeing a cardiologist and having further tests done. They do not have such a specialist at Kingston - which is a bit worrying - and it would mean referral to a teaching hospital like St Thomas's. He said I am still young enough for by-pass surgery if all three of the coronary arteries are affected. Whow!

Meanwhile he sent me home to rest up for a couple of days - and we have our first social engagement booked for today, lunch with the Jacobs at Ascot!

In the event I sat and watched the start of the final Test and, happily, dozed through most of it. Pakistan won the toss and batted all day putting on over three hundred runs.

The doctor has prescribed a nasal spray which finally works. What a relief!

DAY THIRTYNINE

I sat and snoozed most of the day watching the tele. Pakistan spent the time accumulating runs, putting on over 600. They are obviously not interested in a declaration, but seem to be more interested in humiliating England. Who said only white people are racists?

DAY FORTY

I typed hard all day while Sandra cleared out the study. I have a tele in the same room as my computer so that I can keep a beady eye on the Test Match. This was a mistake. Pakistan, determined to put the boot in, scored a massive 708. England followed and shed wickets like confetti.

Cricket has less to do with skill than it has to do with mind and we really should field a psychologist who can bat a bit.

DAY FORTYONE

If anyone could show our cricketers how to think success it must be Nigel Mansell. He is dedicated to it and every fibre of the man is professionally attuned to achieve. Luck always seems to desert the loser in cricket as if an outcome of negative thinking.

Where positive thinking might be the answer for most of our cricketers it is not enough by itself however, for the racing driver. He has to have a good car! Poor Nigel had the Hungarian Grand Prix efficiently buttoned up this afternoon, he was never passed and controlled the race from the front - and then - a wheel nut comes off almost within sight of the flag. What does the poor man have to do to win the championship? Bad luck cannot be a factor of negative thought in Nigel's case where his positive thinking still allows for atrocious luck most of the time.

DAY FORTYTWO

Monday and the start of the second week in August. Everyone is either away on holiday, or just about to go on holiday. It is very depressing sitting here and thinking of them all quaffing vino and slurping huitres in smug self-complacency somewhere in the sun.

Doris White called on her way back from college where she had been to see what the PCAS results were like. Estate Management has recruited on the button, but Quantity Surveying is a bit short. Although confidential at the time of telling me, but it will be public soon, she says she has given in her notice - taking early retirement that is. That will give the Director something else to worry about. The entire leadership in what was the Faculty of Professional Studies to change in a matter of months is a bit of bad management in anyone's book! To lose one head of school is unfortunate, to lose two heads is careless, but to lose three heads, and a dean, is downright wilful!

Doris would have stayed on, she said, if she had been offered the deanship. "Although the thought of trying to cope with that temperamental art and design lot..." She shook her head as if it was too awful to put into words. We then contemplated the sort of problems she would have had - like trying to tell Daphne Brooker there was no more money, or Peter LLoyd-Jones that it was not fashionable anymore to quote the Bauhaus, and the painters that the term started three weeks ago.

But that was unforgivable of us and very disloyal, because we really do love them all, and particularly admire them for their cherished independence. It is that which is going to make life so difficult for the poor sod who eventually has to manage them!

The Test Match goes from bad to worse, with England all out for 232 in their first innings and 95 for three, so far, in their second, still 380 behind.

Jonathan rang from Paris to say he was very drunk, but otherwise well. He should still be in Norway according to his plan. I knew I was right to be worried.

DAY FORTYTHREE

The last day of the Test. Cricket is a remarkable game, one moment it is all gloom and doom, or very boring and suddenly it can change its character and become the most exciting event imaginable. England 380 behind, the last two accredited batsmen in and the whole day to play, not a scenario to keep you gasping. Yet Gatting and Botham played the day through with such amazing dogged application that they denied the Pakistanis the victory they thought they deserved. Gatting made 151 and even more remarkable, Botham only made 51, having batted for umpteen hours with great care and restraint. It really was a demonstration of mind over matter at last!

Ever since I mentioned, a couple of weeks ago, the uniqueness of the Kingston Master's Course in Architectural Design, I have thought that I should elaborate on the statement.

Architecture is usually considered to be a vocational subject and, as such, not popular with some university senates. I think this is indicative of the almost universal misconception about the activity of designing, which at some levels is thought of as a craft skill similar to pottery, or woodwork. I heard a professor of engineering recently refer to designing as drawing, which as he implied, anyone can learn to do. He had relegated the activity in his mind to something akin to an 'O' level subject and was prepared to accord it that sort of importance.

Academic Boards are not the best of places in which to educate professors of engineering. Come to think of it, I am not sure which are the best places - schools of engineering one would have hoped perhaps? Anyway, for the enlightenment of such people then, designing is not a craft skill like drawing, but is an equally intellectual skill - even unto engineering.

By intellect, I mean that faculty of the mind by which one reasons, as distinct from craft skill, by which I mean manual dexterity. In our present society of course, intellectual prowess is favoured over craft skill, but I remind you that it was not always so, not until artists such as Leonardo started assuming airs above their fellow craftsmen. William Morris tried to restore the balance much later of course, with his 'Turn our artists into craftsmen and our craftsmen into artists' credo.

Just how much of a loss is the failure to recognise the value of the craftsman to this age I wonder? Perhaps one could look at the environment for evidence and here I have to castigate all of the professors of engineering, and their ilk, for their philistinism!

But to get back to design as an intellectual skill, the design process is essentially a mental one in which the designer is given a problem to resolve, whether that of a coffee pot or an extension to the National Gallery.

Some design problems may be solvable by the simple application of logic, but rarely are they so easy. Usually there is a conflict of requirements, an either/or situation, where a solution for one aspect is always in conflict with another aspect of the problem. For example, in designing a house which is approached from a road on the north and across which is a magnificent view, while to the south is a dismal outlook on to the gasworks, no amount of logic will get the sun into the room which enjoys the view.

In another field a politician, say, would seek a compromise between the conflicting requirements. A designer however considers compromise as failure and he will always seek a new option, a creative idea to unlock the impasse. He then thrashes around mentally seeking this new option, but unlike the neat flow of reasoning the creative leap cannot be ordered. In fact it most readily happens when you stop trying - like waking up in the morning with the answer to that intractable problem of the night before.

What has happened is that the problem has been referred to the sub-conscious where entirely new connections are made and these then pop up into the conscious domain as something completely different and where the conscious activity of reasoning then immediately starts to check them out for application. This is sometimes called lateral thinking, or inspiration and it follows that the quality of the ideas produced by the sub-conscious will depend upon the quality of the stored knowledge (memories) and the richness with which it has been cultivated.

I remember suggesting to a student while he was struggling to design a fire station, that perhaps he had not identified the real problem, which might have been how to get water to a fire?

The interaction between the conscious and the sub-conscious is fluid, fluent and unfathomable. However it works and at whatever level it works, it is undeniably a cerebral process. It flows cyclically through hypothesis (guess at the solution), test and evaluation, then new hypothesis, re-test and re-evaluation, with occasional hiccups where the requirements are in conflict and reference then has to be made to the sub-conscious for new directions to be suggested, so that the process may continue with fresh hypotheses, and so on.

I find that when I take on a design problem I have to live with it for a period, allowing it to gestate as it were, before I get near the drawing board. The drawing bit is in fact a very advanced stage in the process and only happens when the idea has been formulated enough and is ready to be displayed and evaluated by drawing.

Having identified designing as that familiar process known to scientists as the hypothetico-deductive method, one would have thought it not unreasonable to give it master's degree status. However, as I said earlier, not one polytechnic or university school in this country has succeeded in so doing, not until Kingston, that is.

There are two reasons for this failure, the first due to the need to protect the five-year mandatory grant, and the second due to the failure of anyone to show that designing is sufficiently intellectually rigorous. Kingston disposed of these two snags firstly, by putting the master's on as a part-time course in collaboration with a few carefully selected practices, and secondly, by demonstrating that at Kingston design was sufficiently rigorous as to justify master's status. You must forgive me for being a bit smug about it!

As people like Bill Hillier and Malcolm McKeown have said, architects have generally failed to recognise that their core discipline is design. Architecture has borrowed from many other disciplines over the years, such as technology, science and the social sciences, seemingly under the impression that the grafting of bits of these disciplines on to architecture would make it more academically respectable. A degree in building, or quantity surveying, contains much of this science and technology, but neither a builder nor a quantity surveyor is equipped by their training to design a beautiful piece of architecture.

Architecture is concerned with the organization of form and space and, at the end of the day, to create environments which please - in the words of Sir Henry Wooton, to provide 'Firmness, Commodity and Delight.'

DAY FORTYFOUR

Sandra got in to a heavy typing session today, which went on until mid-afternoon, denying me access to my computer. Now this is meat for domestic discord.

However, harmony was salvaged when Graham Bennett rang. No one can keep up a disagreeable mood for long, having spoken with Graham. He is still off work, poor chap, with his croaked knee. So, we arranged that Sandra would pick him up from the hospital after his physiotherapy session, next Friday.

DAY FORTYFIVE

The new Tesco supermarket opened yesterday and the event of the day had to be a visit. An entertaining way to spend an afternoon, walking around a supermarket? In fact it was quite entertaining, the deli, fish and bakery sections particularly are delightful. It is a great mistake to go food shopping when one is hungry! Driving was particularly bad, whether because patrons had not sussed out the relevant traffic flows, or because they were just tourists like us, I don't know, but I came out with bruised knuckles from unusual trolley bashing.

DAY FORTYSIX

It was great to see Graham here at lunchtime and as the sun was shining, we sat in the patio. Sandra produced a super lunch - Mediterranean Fish Stew with chilled white wine from Howard Martin's Kent vineyard, followed by cabinet pudding and a Muscadet. Howard's Chiddingstone wine is quite delectable; made from the Pinot Gutedel grape, it is one of the finest English wines. I gather that in addition to his British Rail contract, he is also now supplying Westminster.

I have not mentioned Howard's name before; he joined the school in the late sixties and is therefore one of the longest serving members of staff. He originally read philosophy at Cambridge and then architecture at the Bartlett. One of his more notable achievements in the school was to chair the working party which designed the BA degree, which, of course included developing the Electives system, unique in 1972 to Kingston but much copied since and most recently, I gather, by the Bartlett. Howard married one of our diplomates, Mitzi Quirk, who went on to do the MA at Essex, with Joe Rykwert.

Howard is a perfectionist and he worries obsessionally about anything he undertakes until he has it ordered and organized. Even then it is never to his relaxed satisfaction and his burden seems to be that he cannot believe the praise his efforts genuinely earn. He has done a very great deal for the school over the years.

One of Graham Bennett's stories concerned a woman he met on the bus when he was going for hospital treatment. She warned him of the Russian plot whereby they are buying up all the old properties in the country, demolishing them and building office blocks in their place against the day when they invade and take over! She said she had been to the police to warn them and Graham asked her what they had said. The sergeant on the desk had looked at her very seriously and said, "Christ ma'am, we hadn't thought of that!"

DAY FORTYSEVEN

We have acquired another garage on the estate in which I hope to store twenty years worth of files, papers and books from my office at college. I shall need a van to transport it and although the majority of it can be dumped no doubt, I cannot know this without going through it all.

Sandra spent a lot of time transferring stuff from the house and boiler room to the new garage. I hope there will be room for my office papers as well.

For the first time I have experienced the drama of wiping off a day's typing without saving it. Not a pleasant experience and worsened by the fact that I do not really know how it happened.

A neighbour called during the evening to tell us that Alan Ford at 4 Fairacre died last Wednesday. This is the first death we have had on the estate.

DAY FORTYEIGHT

Very tired today and took it easy watching the TV most of the time. Thank heavens, Nigel Mansell won the Austrian Grand Prix, although he nearly crowned himself on a concrete beam standing up in the back of a car on his victory parade. He was later seen holding an ice pack in one hand up to his head and the victory champagne bottle in the other!

DAY FORTYNINE

We saw Carole and Graham unloading their car when we went out shopping. They have had a good holiday it seems and we went round to hear all about it this evening. In the event we heard more of Stewart's efforts to look after himself while they were away. He discovered cooking, which appeared to have occupied him from the moment he got home in the evening and until he went to bed. He has failed one of his three "A" levels and is now worried about getting in to University, poor lad.

DAY FIFTY

Rudolf Hess died yesterday in Spandau, in slightly odd circumstances. He was found with a cord around his neck and a suicide type of note. One does not commit suicide however, simply by tying a cord around one's throat. Perhaps it was psychosomatic in that he thought he was killing himself, and did!

Hess never fired my imagination as the other Nazi leaders did, although I do remember his arrival in Scotland in a Messerschmitt 110 fighter plane on 10th May 1941. I had volunteered for pilot training in the RAF some six months earlier and was waiting to be called up.

At the time I was less interested in the reason for his flight and far more interested in the fact that he had brought one of those ME's over intact for us to inspect. There were quite a few remains scattered over the Kent countryside already, of course. It transpired that his flight to this country from Augsburg, the private airfield of the Messerschmitt company, caused Hitler acute embarrassment at the time. Messerschmitt's immediate arrest was ordered, as was that of dozens of Hess's staff, but unfortunately the brilliant aeroplane designer was cleared of complicity and released to carry on his own war against the Allies.

An Air Vice Marshall, I think his name was Ivor Bloom, was being interviewed the other morning on LBC and reference was made to Hess's flight. I was surprised to hear this illustrious gentleman talk about it being made in a light aircraft. No way could the twin-engined ME 110 be called a light aircraft.

When I say the Nazi leaders fired my imagination, I mean in a morbidly curious way, as they did for millions of other people as well. That was the nature of their power after all.

When Albert Speer was released from Spandau I wrote and invited him to Kingston in his role as an architect rather than a Nazi leader. His neo-classical designs for Berlin, including his design for the Great Hall and the Arch of Triumph in the proposed New Centre for Berlin, were not great architecture, but they were of immense interest in their grandiose monumentality. In any case I would dearly have loved to meet one of those horrendous men from that devilish coven. He replied saying that he would be delighted to visit us, but only if the RIBA would receive him as well. I think this was an understandable proviso and I happily asked the President if he could arrange something, only to be told that it was not on - a typically inept RIBA response!

I visited Knights Park for the first time since my attack, this afternoon. My office was locked and Harri told me that he was keeping it that way until I returned to clear it. It reminded me of Miss Haversham of 'Great Expectations' fame.

DAY FIFTYONE

The results of the 24-hour ECG were available today and Dr Gunraj, at the hospital, explained that they showed occasional atrial and ventrical ectopic beats, or extra heart beats. Until recently these beats were thought to be dangerous, but now it is known their effect on the heart's performance is minimal, or so he says! Anyway, he does not propose doing anything further for a month, until the heart has settled down after the heart attack. There are drugs available to control the ectopic beats and I am already having propranolol which controls the atrial variety. But the drug for the ventrical beats has side effects, like retention of urine, and I can do without that. These extra beats are felt like a thud in the chest and can make one feel dizzy. Most people have them to an extent, apparently, and they can be made more evident with strong coffee or tea.

Now that you have had your attention drawn to these extra beats and thuds in the chest, you should be able to imagine you have them if you think hard enough, OK?

DAY FIFTYTWO

A great cricketing occasion, the 200th anniversary of the MCC, celebrated by a game of cricket to end all cricket, MCC versus the Rest of the World. Gatting leads the MCC team and Alan Border the rest, and what teams they are.

I invited Harri, my Faculty Administrative Officer, to lunch and to view the start of the game on the tele. It is very fortunate that Sandra loves cricket as much as I do and is therefore as keen as I am to watch it. We had a delightful lunch of Salmon and Prawn Lasagne, followed by fresh fruit and cheese. Unfortunately the Orvieto I had chosen was very cloudy and we had to revert to a Lambrusco, which was really too sweet for the event. I guess I was trying to be too clever with my lasagne and Italian wines. However, the cricket was magnificent, Gooch making a comeback with 117 and Gatting, by the end of the day, not out 157. But it was not just the unfamiliar sight of Englishmen scoring runs that made it entertaining, the general atmosphere of the game was so enjoyable and completely without needle.

The new roof on the Mound Stand, a series of tensile canvas tents, looks very jolly and seems to be approved by everyone. I would have liked to see them a bit larger and less timid perhaps, but all praise to the MCC for their choice of architect - Michael Hopkins.

DAY FIFTYTHREE

The entertainment from Lord's continues, Gatting finally making 179 and then declaring at 455 for 5 wickets. What a sight, Marshall and Imran Khan bowling to Haynes, Vengsarkar, Border and Gavaskar! The little Indian batsman announced his retirement from first class cricket at the beginning of this match and like Imran Khan he will probably never be seen again playing cricket in this country. He went on to score 80 by the end of the day and although he holds most of the batting records, he has never scored a century at Lord's. Will he be able to score his hundred tomorrow? Watch this space.

We tore ourselves from the television at the tea interval and went in to Bentalls to collect my 'long service award' from the Royal Borough. I was informed of this award by letter last July which went like this:

> "I write to advise you that by virtue of your 25 years' service with the Royal Borough since 1/1/62 you are entitled to a gift to the value of £75 (exclusive of VAT) or a cash gift of £75 (which is subject to income tax). The gift entitlement, being exclusive of VAT means that the Council will meet the cost of a gift whose value does not exceed £86.25, this sum being inclusive of VAT. You may select a gift to a higher value than the amount of the award, but the Council will only pay the amount stated above. You should pay any additional amount direct to the supplier ..."

The letter went on like this for one and a half pages, finishing with what I hope was a typing error,

"... in the meantime I would like to take this opportunity to thank you for your local service to the Royal Borough."

I like to think that my service was more on a regional scale, if not downright national - or do you think they meant *loyal?*

It was a nice idea ruined by administrative incompetence. The letter should have been signed by the Chairman of the Education Committee at least, or the Mayor even and certainly not by a clerk. In any case it would have been better had it sounded as if it were making an award for long service - and not a fine for a parking offence. Local bloody government!

It took us the rest of the afternoon to extract my 'award' out of Bentalls. Armed with the letter from the Royal Borough which said *"Your award is now ready for collection from Bentalls."*, we presented it to the counter which sells telephones. They said, "We aren't Bentalls. We are British Telecom."

So we went up to the top floor to Customer Enquiries. They said, "Oh yes, go down to the counter marked British Telecom." We said we have just come from there. "Ah." and she went off to make further enquiries.

She came back and said far too confidently, "We haven't actually received the paperwork, but I have spoken to the Borough and if you now go down to British Telecom you can collect your gift."

It was a different girl at British Telecom. She did not know anything about a long service award. I explained that Customer Enquiries had said she would know all about it. She tried to understand and listened hard. "What has a Bentalls long service award got to do with the Borough?"

I could see her problem. I began to have my doubts too. So, I tried to explain it all once again - patiently. It was when she pointed out that they were British Telecom and not Bentalls that I began to lose interest. Fortunately the girl I had first spoken to came back and rekindled hope. She suggested they rang Customer Enquiries. I should have thought of that. Obviously Customer Enquiries made sense, because she went off and got a large box with an Answer Phone in it. But we weren't quite there yet.

"I shall have to put your letter in the till," she said. "You can't do that," I said, "It's my award letter."

Sandra suggested they photocopied it. The two girls looked around like hunted animals. Then one of them picked up the letter and wandered off, presumably to look for a photocopying machine. She failed to find one.

Her voice was very little as she explained she couldn't find one. They had had a very hard day, you could tell. Sandra suggested they used the fax machine on the counter. "After all, you do sell fax machines," she said.

That was unkind of her. They had to get the manual to see how it worked and when they had finally sorted it out, it printed my letter diagonally across the sheet.

DAY FIFTYFOUR

A storm and heavy rain during the night should have stopped the cricket, but amazingly, they actually started play at 11.30.

The commentators had quite a chunter about if this were a Test Match the umpires would have been in and out of the pavilion like Jacks-in-the-box with the outfield too wet for play until mid-afternoon. But being the sort of game it is, with everyone having a good time, they are prepared to play. It does go to show what is possible, even on a wet outfield.

So, while Sandra went shopping, I watched the cricket and what cricket it is too. What better entertainment could one wish for than seeing Marshall and Hadlee bowling to Gavaskar and Imran Khan? Gavaskar made his century, his first at Lords, to everyone's delight, but unfortunately the rain returned and washed the game away in the afternoon.

We entertained Jenny and Jane to lunch, Jenny being Sandra's stepmother. Jane, who is into computing, tried to penetrate some of my software for me, but without success. It is fascinating though to watch a computer buff working away; they seem to have a close understanding with the machine which is almost telepathic. At my first 'syntax error' or 'bad command' I simply freeze.

The trip in to Bentalls last Friday to collect my long service award and the resulting fight with the road works and traffic chaos reminded me of one of my particular hates - Traffic Managers or Planners. It was probably Colin Buchanan who first fed the notion to me in his report, Traffic in Towns, but it is one that I have nurtured and developed over the years ever since. Roads breed traffic. Without roads there would be no traffic, it is as simple as that. I wrote in a paper I gave in the early seventies about the environment,

'Building bigger and better roads for the motorcar has often been challenged by the environmentalists as a dubious policy, one of palliative rather than solution, or as in the words of Palmerston, 'like feeding cutlets to a tiger.'

The motorcar is insatiable and will gobble up every new road it is offered, as the brave new M25 demonstrates. x traffic uses an existing road, albeit ungraciously but it does keep moving along. Then the traffic engineer builds a bigger and better road which should allow x traffic to move more freely. But it doesn't and within weeks conditions are as bad as they were on the old road, because x traffic is now x + y traffic. The new road has generated more traffic, and it will continue to do this until conditions reach the near limit once more and you are back to the original level of traffic flow.

The near limit, or what I term the 'near saturation factor', is an important measure. Whatever the demand upon an urban road system the traffic rarely seizes up completely. The first time it ever happened was in Kingston some few years ago. It was a Saturday afternoon and Kingston centre was full with its normal weekend shoppers. A sudden storm and downpour sent the shoppers scuttling for their cars. Within minutes the traffic in the middle of Kingston froze solid and no one could move. It took the police and wardens an hour or so to release the thrombosis. However, this was not an example of traffic saturation in the sense I am using the expression here. Just so much traffic comes on to a given road system as will permit it to keep moving, albeit very slowly. It seems that before the point where the traffic might remorselessly lock up, newly entering traffic bleeds away and a very delicate balance of near saturation is maintained.

It is pointless to ask where the new traffic comes from each time because we all want to use our car. It is also pointless to think that one could ever build enough roads to satisfy demand. Stand on the concourse at Waterloo Station one morning and watch the human tide flood in from the trains and think of the road acreage you would need to take the cars to carry that lot! London would become one vast motorway. It is said that only 20% of London commuters come in by car and there is simply not enough space to build the roads which would accommodate even a fraction of the remainder.

The fact is that we can never have enough roads in any urban situation to satisfy the demand. There will always be more traffic trying to use whatever roads are provided than can be accommodated. Thus there will always be traffic congestion. The amount of the congestion will be determined not by the amount of traffic wanting to use the road, but by the amount of traffic the road can take.

It is the failure to understand this last fact that befuddles the thinking of traffic managers. Impelled by the apparent threat that the traffic will go on increasing past the saturation point they vainly hope to satisfy the demands of the vociferous roads lobby but fail to see that this will always be impossible. And the really big disaster area for all traffic managers/planners is - quality of environment!

If your ulcer-generator is traffic flow then one does not stop to think too long about houses, pedestrians and the like. They are embarrassments which get in the way of your progress. Colin Buchanan's proposals in the late sixties, while still too radical for most people today, were really inadequate then. He advocated a road hierarchy where local roads fed into through-service roads, but I believe that even he overlooked the 'insatiability' factor. His through-service roads would soon have become 'near saturated' making his design as unworkable as any traffic planner's will always become.

I was delighted to read today that Dr Martin Mogridge, of the transport studies group at University College, seems to be in total agreement with me. He says - and I quote from the magazine of the Institute of Civil Engineers - "By easing congestion and speeding traffic flows, highway authorities bring more people on to the roads. That restores the congestion and reduces the number of people using buses and trains. Services are cut and more people use their own transport."

'Dear Dr Mogridge, I fear that you are baying at the moon and no one will hear you. The road and road haulage lobbies have long since deafened the public with their raucous demands for bigger and better roads.'

What intrigues me, not only as an architect but also as a fact of history, is our over-preoccupation with this new artefact, the motorcar. Mankind for thirty thousand years has been building shelters for himself and the wife and kids. The Mammoth hunters killed that great beast, skinned it, ate the meat and then draping its skeleton with leaves, moved in - le premier Chez Nous?

The activity of building shelter has gone on ever since, becoming a fundamental feature of humanity and has marked one society from another down the ages. Thousands of years ago, nomadic tribes in central Asia developed a transportable tent called a Yurt, a system just like garden trelliswork. The Eskimo's Igloo has been around quite a long time too, to say nothing of the African Grass Houses, the Indians' Tepee, the Mexicans' Pueblo, the Mandans' Lodge, the Bedouins' Tent, the Italian Trullo house, the Dogon house in Timbuktu, right up to the archetypal English house - half-timbered with wattle and daub infilling and a thatched roof.

We are at the end of an epoch of centuries of building and of creating communities, collections of homes and public buildings which had reached an advanced level of urbanity even 2000 years ago. How great was the sophistication employed by Hausman say, in laying out the vistas of Paris - and yet without a motorcar in sight!

The motorcar, traffic flows, motorways, all of these have only happened in the last five minutes. Suddenly, overnight it seems, we are having to cope with this monstrous invasion of the tin box on wheels which is literally tearing out the heart of thousands of years of urban development. We naturally cling to the community life form we have inherited, the urban pattern, and why shouldn't we? But now we have to graft this mobile tin status symbol in to the classical urban texture - and it simply does not fit!

Look at what happened to Detroit. The car moved in and people finally had to move out. That is downright stupid.

I think it is particularly stupid too when one remembers that it is a transport system based upon a finite energy source - oil. The fossil fuels are our smallest reserve and yet we are using them at the highest rate in the forms of coal and oil. It is said that they are too valuable to burn anyway as they serve as the basis of much of our chemical industry. Each year of our present power consumption took three million years to accumulate, and that is one hell of a statistic! Mr Micawber would have done his nut. Lord Robens, former chairman of the National Coal Board, as far back as 1974 was calling for an International Energy Council. Now, thirteen years later, our apathy knows no limits. We are vigorously doing nothing.

For the last thirty odd years, planners have been trying to come to terms with the motorcar, accepting its virtues of freedom and mobility as if sacred. More recently however, these virtues have become decidedly more illusory than real. Car ownership in the thirties was considerably lower than it is today, but the standard of life in environmental terms was much higher. The corner shop, local delivery services, public transport even, have all been eroded by mass car ownership. The car spawned the hypermarket with its dramatic reduction in personal service.

How ironic it will be if the planners, by force majeure, have to plan for a society without the motorcar. Public transport systems, for a start, would have to be upgraded - at whatever the cost. I suggest that the effects of the energy crisis, when it bites, will emerge as the one single item most dramatically to change the fabric of our urban life.

The road lobby will have to develop another way of propelling its vehicles soon if it is to keep them on the road, so to speak, in the next century.

I will hazard another guess though about that; I believe there will be a drift away from personalised transport in urban situations and certainly in inter-city travel, even if some form of personal transport will always be necessary in rural locations. Any overview of fuels suggests that the future of energy production will show a trend towards power being produced centrally and relayed to the consumer, rather than fuel being available to the consumer for local conversion into energy.

In other words, electrical power, however produced centrally will more and more replace locally consumed fossil fuels. I do not think that it will be in my time, but I believe that Jonathan will see the underground considerably extended and even the reintroduction of tramways, if not your actual moving pavements. The point here is that electric power generation, based upon a small number of large machines, reaches a thermal efficiency of 40%, while the transport industry using a large number of small machines only achieves an efficiency averaging at 25%.

Surely it would be more sensible, in the light of these arguments to preserve our urban structures and to expend our invention and energy upon developing more sophisticated, comfortable and exciting forms of public transport, and to reduce the emphasis upon the urban motorcar, so that when the oil finally runs out, we don't have to revert to the horse - I'm allergic to manure anyway!

104

DAY FIFTYFIVE

Up late - 10 o'clock! It is Sunday after all and this is the first lie-in we have had. Anyway, I felt tired.

I typed until mid-afternoon and then we went for a walk, calling in on Carole and Graham for a cup of tea, on the way home. They make me feel vaguely guilty with their DIY industry, as they paint the outside of their house. I wonder if I will ever be able to do anything really strenuous again like that. Some may well welcome the excuse not to, but I would be most unhappy.

I come from a family of DIY enthusiasts who were into the activity long before it was a national disease. I never knew my father employ anyone to do a job in the house and he was teaching me woodwork and metalwork soon after I got out of nappies. His joy was in the attempting though, rather than the completing. He was not a very good finisher and the quality of some of his enterprises left a bit to be desired. Enterprise was the key word and he was greatly admired for it, except perhaps by mother. I think she was overly critical of his workmanship, but it never diminished my father's enthusiasm for pottering one jot.

DAY FIFTYSIX

Sandra went to Channing first thing this morning, to do a spot of work for the Head and leaving me to watch the resumption of the MCC Centenary Match. Gatting declared at 318 for 6 wickets, Gooch having made 70 of them and Greenidge 122. Poor Sunil Gavaskar was bowled for a duck, but the pavilion still stood for him as he came in.

Jon rang from Paris. He is leaving for Spain tomorrow. He was very impressed by Denmark apparently and said he could easily work there.

DAY FIFTYSEVEN
We had decided to go to Norfolk today, but the weather is so awful, very cold and pissing down with rain. Not only was Norfolk abandoned but the cricket as well, a sad ending to such a memorable match.

However, the gloom was momentarily lifted by a telephone call from the Borough.

"British Telecom would like to know when you are going in to collect your Answering Machine?"

"I collected it last Friday."

"Ooo-er. What are they on about?"

I told her I could not imagine and I explained about the difficulties we had had between Bentalls and British Telecom.

"But if they would like me to have another one I will happily call and collect it."

She agreed and suggested I give the second one to her.

DAY FIFTYEIGHT
The weather report is still bad for East Anglia, rain, rain, rain. In the hope that it still might improve, we took the car to have its MOT, having discovered when we tried to tax it that it had just expired.

We called in at Knights Park on the way home and made a start on clearing out my drawers and cupboards. Having filled one monster waste bin which the caretaker had thoughtfully provided we decided that it would do for starters.

I met Don Priest in the car park, the Polytechnic Safety Officer, and we compared data on heart attacks. He has had two and now takes things extremely slowly. That was his very firm advice to me too. I don't think the medics would entirely agree, although I would not argue with Don. I cannot take anything but slowly!

DAY FIFTYNINE

While not actually raining it is cold and dismal. Sandra started off by getting things organised for the trip to Norfolk, but I said that I really did not feel up to it. I cannot yet contemplate sitting in the car for three hours and then having the hassle of finding a suitable hotel at this point in time.

My biggest adventure so far has been the shopping trip to Cheam, all of fifteen minutes drive away. Just getting myself together and into the car is exhausting enough, without the drive itself.

I am a very bad passenger at the best of times and I hate being driven by others. I assume that one is not allowed to drive for at least two months following a heart attack because of the strain it imposes. However, I think it is highly questionable to suppose it is any less of a strain to be driven. My feet nearly go through the floor as I press on phantom pedals and I am never fully convinced that we will miss all the parked cars. The strain of not offering advice to the driver all the time must be worse than doing it myself, to say nothing of the strain upon Sandra!

DAY SIXTY

We went in to college again having remembered that I officially retire on Monday and that thereafter I will be trespassing. We made a good inroad upon packing stuff in to boxes and loading the car to its gunwales.

I say we ... I should say Sandra, I merely supervise.

She has become hooked on genealogy and has spent lots of time these last two years searching our two family trees. It started when she set out to prove, or otherwise, the claim that Admiral Sir Edward Berry was an ancestor. The Berrys have always made this claim, supported by the fact that the last two generations at least were all seafaring folk. My father would happily tell the story of how he was lashed to the mast of granddad's boat for six hours in a hurricane. The story was a bit of family mythology and no doubt had its truth buried in it somewhere. It certainly was true that his brother Victor went to the South Pole in the Discovery, with Shackleton, because we have the photographs to prove it. I am perhaps less convinced about Sir Edward. It is a fact that, according to his portrait in the Dulwich Art Gallery, he did have the Berry beak, the large proboscis, which we all handsomely sport! He was ennobled after the Battle of the Nile, I believe, following Nelson's good account of his deeds. He then became Nelson's Captain on his Flagship and also commanded the Agamemnon at Trafalgar.

Sandra is convinced that she will prove it, but the final bit of conclusive evidence evades her. These histories do become murky, if not opaque, after you get beyond the first Census of 1800 and something! But she has spent time in situ, as it were, in Norfolk, perusing parish records and has even got involved corresponding with people in the States and in Australia.

She went off to the Records Office this afternoon. I think it is the detection process, the search for and pursuit of intangible clues, which appeals to her. She enjoys Agatha Christie too.

I got hooked upon "Close Encounters of the Third Kind" on the box and sat up until after one o'clock. A very large spider however, chose the climax of the film to walk across my feet and I spent the next five minutes hunting for it, so I don't know how it finished. What with the spider and the moronic characters in the film, I think I would have been better off with an early night.

DAY SIXTYONE

Sandra sorted out the study and took lots of Open University scripts and books over to the garage. In the process she dug my old bicycle out of storage and gave it a service. She called me out to try it and I drove it round the estate. It is great fun, much less effort than walking. Sandra visualizes me going off to get the bread every morning - and why not?

One's driving licence is mandatorily suspended for at least two months following a heart attack and this period is up on Monday.

I have my letter ready and waiting to send to the DVLC. We have been talking about changing the car meanwhile, as it has seemed inappropriate for Sandra to do the shopping in a large, thirsty Mercedes. She wants a small hatchback like a Golf, she says. However, I would like something a bit more exciting than that.

We saw a Volvo 480 ES parked at the kerb the other day, a most un-Volvo looking car and I was prompted to follow it up with the local Volvo agents. We went to inspect it today. It has only been around for about a month and I was very impressed. It is an estate with strong sporty overtones but whether these extend beyond mere styling remains to be proven.

I insist on a bit of individuality with my motorcars, a bit of character. There aren't many British cars unfortunately which still display such qualities. My early 60's E type Jaguar certainly did, as did my Morgan 4.4 and the Reliant Scimitar GT. But other than these British masterpieces I have had to buy foreign, like my two Porsches and the Citroen DS. Now there was a beautiful car, the Citroen DS, styled like the old Morphy Richards flat iron, or was it the other way round? If only it was still in production, I would buy it above all else. Incredibly comfortable, fast, effortless to drive and crammed with character.

Compare it to any of today's offerings from Longbridge. How can British car designers get it so wrong for so long? I have to exclude Colin Chapman, the Broadley cousins (of Lola fame), Jem Marsh and a few others from this blanket gripe which does really centre upon the mass-produced family monstrosities produced by the big British factories rather than the much smaller enterprises like Lotus, TVR, Gemini, Reliant, AC, Morgan, etc. These latter manufacturers show that it can be done in this country and that we are not devoid of design talent.

The malaise is a general one and not restricted to the motor industry of course. It has everything to do with British management being totally oblivious to the role of design in manufacture. Thank heavens there does appear to be some improvement these days, but progress is so painfully slow that

I sometimes wonder if the penny took too long to drop and that it is happening now - all too late!

As a student I used to go to Denmark and wonder at the standard of design of everything in the shops, and again in Italy. Not for the peasants are there three flying ducks across the wall, or the cream and green decor, or the grotesque gnome sitting in the municipal-type flowerbed in the front garden. It is fashionable today of course, to excuse such poverty of taste and absence of design appreciation by talking about freedom, self-expression and personalisation. Personalisation, Pillocks! If someone has nothing to say to me, other than that he is visually illiterate, it would be better if he kept quiet. I would have him resist his urge to self-express at the risk of mortal constipation!

In my irritation at the appalling level of design appreciation in this country generally I must not become too extreme in my argument. There is after all an increasing understanding of the role of symbolism, particularly in architecture where, for example, the meaning of 'house' conveys a much more loaded message than was fully understood by the so -called rational architects of the Modern Movement. Indeed it was this failure which resulted in people finally rejecting Corbusier's dictum about the house being a machine to live in as well as the whole style of architecture that went with it. This was a case of throwing the baby out with bath water though, because there is nothing wrong with being rational, nothing wrong that is - as long as you temper it with a bit of poetry, as indeed did Corb!

Corbusier is about to be rediscovered, of course. We have had the Corb Exhibition at the Haywood and we are now due for the great revival. Good - except the revivalists will get him all wrong with Corbusian pastiche I am quite sure.

111

However, there is a danger that the average architect today is going too far with this post-modernism bit. They usually do go over the top in these matters, which brings me back to an earlier gripe - fashion in architecture. If they do go too far they will run the risk of creating functionally inadequate buildings as they did in Japan apparently, where they built light-weight, southern type houses - which were symbolic of the modern southern culture - in the north! The occupants shivered to death.

They are certainly in hazard of creating inappropriate buildings, like Venturi's urban house in America - with a Swiss farmhouse roof. A dose of rationalism here might have been relevant? Oh dear, come back Corb, all is forgiven.

I must say I am sick to death of red paint, which seems to be the only colour known, or permitted to post-modern architects - that and red plastic tubing which serves as post-modern ironmongery - more like Jacques Tati every day! An appropriate name for post-modern architecture, in addition to Disneyland, would be - the Toyshop style.

DAY SIXTYTWO

My first real outing, we went to Peter and Lesley's for lunch at Sunningdale. Lesley made a super lunch - Dublin Bay Prawns followed by chicken in a delicious mushroom sauce and of course, Howard's Chiddingstone wine.

The prime quality which every one at Kingston possessed was loyalty, both to me as well as to the school. John Farmer was offered a tutorship at Cambridge a few years ago, and in spite of it being the academics' Mecca, he turned it down saying he could not leave Kingston. Tim Bell was offered a personal chair at Cardiff and he too turned this down.

But when I talk of loyalty I have to place Peter at the top of the tree. He joined me a few years after I became head, a relatively new first class honours graduate from Newcastle, keen and immensely efficient. He started as a part-timer, but quickly demonstrated a natural talent for teaching and I gave him a lectureship. Peter has served in pretty well every role there is in the school, teaching in all years, co-ordinating the technology courses, lecturing conservation and theory and even co-ordinating Professional Practice, a role reserved for only the most senior and experienced member of staff. As deputy head, during my five years as dean of faculty, he practically ran the school, timetabling, staffing, resources and dealing with the minute-by-minute problems which 230 students constantly create.

What I now realise is that I expected everything to continue going right in the school, and when it did it was no cause for comment. It was only when things went wrong that I would shout at Peter, like for example when I found that he had nodded through a higher number than was normal of students transferring to other courses, or simply dropping out, without keeping me informed. I did that because I was being chased by the Academic Board - so, why should I suffer for Peter's misdeeds? What a terrible way that was to repay his loyalty to me!

"Ah well. I am wearing a hair shirt, Peter, and I am very contrite."

Michael and Sue have got back safely from their holiday in France. He christened our answering machine while we were at Sunningdale, leaving a daft message on it. I had begun to wonder whether the stupid thing worked and was relieved to get his 'bleeping' message.

DAY SIXTYTHREE

This is Monday, the start of a new week, it is also the August Bank Holiday and it is the last day of my working life. I retire at midnight! The significance of the last item is that I will no longer have a salary coming in, only a pension.

If I hadn't had that bloody heart attack we would be moving down to Devon about now and getting into a lather over the barn conversion. Sod it! Instead, we spent the day dead-filing lots of papers in the study and transferring them to the garage. As fast as we make space, however, we fill it up with more books and papers from college. My retirement seems to have released an avalanche of paper.

During our walk this afternoon to get Sandra's new season ticket from the station, I noticed these holes in the pavement. They are quite regularly spaced suggesting that they are by design rather than by accident. Each hole precisely takes the ferrule of my walking stick, which is how I first noticed them really. I was walking on leaving my stick upright in the pavement behind me. I have seen these holes in other places before today, but have never stopped to question them.

Being an architect I am quite used to the sight of bore holes, which are bigger of course, and the holes made by wood eating beetles. They are smaller. These pavement holes are somewhere in between the two. I am unaware of any creature capable of eating tarmacadam, so I assume the holes are not formed by insects.

Nor are they created by stiletto heels in hot weather, as nice an explanation as that might have been, because it was not hot. In any case no girl would have that big a stride - particularly wearing stiletto heels. So, what causes them? Who does this pavement pecking?

It must be a nocturnal enterprise, otherwise people would see whatever, or whoever, is responsible and no one I have ever spoken to has seen it/them. Someone told me it was the gasmen who did it, but I know he was having a clever guess. Too clever in fact, which I knew when he started talking about these gasmen jumping about on pogo sticks. No one could jump that far on a pogo stick, and anyway, why the hell should gasmen go jumping up and down Acacia Grove on pogo sticks at 10-foot centres? It doesn't make sense. If it's gas they are after, they would be better off with sniffer dogs, or canaries.

DAY SIXTYFOUR

The first day of my retirement and Sandra goes back to work. The morning was endless. I made the mistake I suppose of getting up to see her off at 7.30.

I had breakfast, read the paper, did the Times Portfolio, attempted the crossword, which was far too hard, and then typed for what I thought was the rest of the day. It was only just 12 o'clock! I don't think I shall be able to survive this retirement bit.

I did survive the afternoon however, and went up to meet Sandra off her train and together we then went for me to get signed off by the doctor. Dr Sherski was on holiday but Dr Flight saw me. He was not into my case history and wanted to know what was wrong with me.

"I've had a heart attack, doctor."

He didn't even blink. Really hardened men, these doctors. He handed me my final certificate saying, "I wish you a happy retirement Mr Berry."

"I hope it's a long one." I said.

DAY SIXTYFIVE

If anything is designed to give one a heart attack, letters from the Inspector of Taxes must rate top. I had one this morning. The day that I am notified of my superannuation lump sum the Inspector of Taxes has to write and claw some of it back as capital gains. What exquisite judgement; they must have courses in how to do it!

I went out shopping today for the first time by myself; up New Malden High Street and I did the rounds including the fishmonger's where he persuaded me to take two fillets of plaice. Sandra asked me why I had bought cod fillets for supper?

The camera shop was a bit more successful perhaps. I have been waiting about four months for them to get me a dedicated cable to enable me to operate the flashgun away from the camera. The last time I enquired they were making noises like - no longer in production. This time the lad looked a bit puzzled and told me that I didn't need a dedicated cable at all and who was daft enough to tell me I did in the first place and that all I need is a gadget to clip on the top of the camera which they always have available in stock anyway, etc, etc.

Jonathan rang from Barios da Luna, northern Spain, to say he was just about to leave for the south. He is meeting up with a couple of his friends who have rented a villa near Malaga. It is quite an itinerary he has kept to so far, with San Tropez next stop in a week or so where he is to stay with more friends up in the hills near Plan de la Tour. After that it will be Milan where he is to stay as a guest of Alfa Romeo. He wrote to them months ago to say he had bought an ancient Spyder which was in need of a complete rebuild. He asked them if they could do this at the factory, saying he would drive it out and would do any job for them - like sweeping the factory floors, while they worked on his car. His letter must have touched a responsive PR cord with the higher management at Alfa's, because he had an amazingly nice letter back. They said that while they could not rebuild his Spyder at Milan they would be very happy to show him around the factory if he would like to go out and stay in the entertainment suite at their hotel.

The original Alfa Spyder is a very sweet car and I do understand Jon's passion for it. I mentioned once to him that I would not mind getting one for myself. He said - and he meant it - "I would never speak to you again if you got a Spyder better than mine."

I have to go for a barium meal tomorrow, to check on the status of my ulcer, so no food after midnight! Who the hell eats after midnight anyway?

DAY SIXTYSIX

We got to the hospital at nine o'clock - along with about fifteen other people, all with nine o'clock appointments. It really is too bad and requires so little administrative effort to space appointments out a bit and yet hospitals are notorious for this abuse. I remember, when Jonathan was a baby, having a hospital appointment for him and having to wait over an hour before anything happened. In the end I demanded the name and address of the Chairman of the Governing Board of the hospital. We were seen within three minutes!

We, the British public, do not complain nearly enough. I had to go in to the local DHSS office quite recently and was appalled by the length of the queue and the slowness of the only counter assistant dealing with it. I asked to see the supervisor. When this person appeared, a formidable creature of indeterminate age - and sex, I informed her - loudly - that we were not sheep to be herded and that as a servant of the public it was her duty to see that the queue was kept moving as expeditiously as possible. Within minutes there were five counter assistants working.

When I finally got in to the business end of the barium meal the radiologist, who the nurses called doctor, stared at me and said, "Oh, you're Mr Berry." Now that set me back a bit. I hadn't been complaining, or threatening to call the chairman, or anything. I was the perfect submissive patient. He said that he remembered my bowels at the New Victoria Hospital some three or four years ago ... A very impressive performance of memory.

He took about a dozen pictures of my belly and the nurses were pinning them up on an illuminated screen as fast as they were produced. I recognised my duodenal (one does get to know these things with experience) and I was not at all happy about the great splodgy, lumpy size of it. I stopped looking.

I was on was a rotating table with the x-ray gadget hovering over the top, the whole lot being totally manoeuvrable. The x-ray thing had a pyramidal base to it which at one stage he swooped down towards my side. He missed however, from his safe remote control position, and bashed it into my lower ribs. It made me squeal.

Bloody x-rays aren't supposed to be painful, but that session would have been better with an anaesthetic!

After the hospital appointment this morning there is nothing in my diary for a couple of weeks. This is the most notable thing about retirement so far, the escape from the tyranny of the diary. It is a blessed relief I have discovered, not to have every hour of one's day prescribed by that beastly book. Ever since I bought my Filofax sometime in the late fifties, yes thirty years ago, it has chased me from one endless meeting to another, thousands of them. I wonder what would have happened to the world had I missed them all?

DAY SIXTYSEVEN

Harri rang and suggested that he and Debbie took me out to lunch. Debbie has hired a car for the week to move her stuff into her new flat. She passed her driving test quite recently so her driving skills are not too polished as yet, but she is a very determined and accomplished young lady and things like that do not put her off. As we drove up to the Royal Oak she told me how another car had smashed off her driving mirror as she drove passed it, spraying her with glass. I walked back from the pub. Well, she was facing in the right direction for college and it seemed unnecessary to put her to the bother of turning round. I needed the exercise anyway.

I walked up to the post office after lunch and opened an investment account with my superannuation lump sum. It was the biggest cheque I have ever written, £25,000. The counter assistant dealt with it as if it happened every day. Perhaps it does.

DAY SIXTYEIGHT

My ribs are very painful. It wouldn't surprise me if that x-ray cameraman had cracked one the other day!

No Indian Summer this year, the weather is the pits! It is very wet and cold, too wet to go shopping in Kingston market as we had hoped to do. So we drove to our new Tesco Super Store and shopped there, along with 13,000,000 others, give or take the odd trolley.

Here I am, living on a pittance of a pension and I have just ordered a new camera. I feel thoroughly guilty about it. It isn't as if I don't have a camera already, because I do, a very expensive Nikon. The new one is a Nikon too, also very expensive. No way can I possibly justify it. Well, how does this sound?

My original camera, a thirty-year old Pentax which I used for colour - keeping the Nikon for real photography - needed a service, the shutter hiccupped every so often. The dealer offered me 30% off the price of the new Nikon camera body in part exchange for the Pentax and that, plus the cost of servicing the Pentax, practically pays for the new Nikon. I will now have two camera bodies sharing my Nikon lenses, instead of two cameras with half a dozen lenses - much less to carry around. I think that all sounds very convincing. Why do I feel so guilty then?

In the excitement of looking at new cameras, (don't you find them exquisite pieces of engineering?) I forgot my aching ribs, not that I offer this in anyway as a justification.

DAY SIXTYNINE

Sandra withdrew all day to battle with my accounts for the tax return. She was at it until 11 pm, what a way to spend a Sunday!

In days of yore my accounts were prepared by an illustrious firm of accountants called Ball Baker Carnaby and

Deed and the man who actually dealt with them was a Mr Cox. I first went to him twenty-five or thirty years ago when it was a very small set up and he was the senior man. He always gave me a friendly and personal service. As time passed the firm expanded and grew although I was never actually aware of this as Mr Cox carried on handling my accounts. It was not until he died a few years ago and the organisation took his place that I became aware of the present scale of the enterprise. It had grown over the years to a vast business and I realized what an incredible service Mr Cox had been giving me. As a senior partner in this international organization he had continued right up to his death to deal personally with my tu'penny ha'penny private account.

With this realization I did not have the gall to carry on using such a massive firm and it was at that stage that Sandra took over. The amazing thing was that although she knew absolutely nothing about tax law, or income tax returns and relied solely upon the occasional telephone call to the tax inspector, she succeeded in getting me tax rebates year after year. Perhaps it is like house conveyancing, there is less to it than we are led to believe?

It occurred to me that I now have time to develop those dozens of films that have been accumulating recently. I picked one at random and having mixed fresh chemicals went through the process, taking a couple of hours all together I suppose. It turned out to be the film I shot of the barn at Boss Hill. An unkind coincidence!

DAY SEVENTY
I have not received any redirected mail from college since I had my attack. I have often thought they are being too protective

because I did get quite a lot of personal mail. It cannot all have suddenly dried up the very day I stopped going in. For the first time four letters arrived today having been redirected - two were junk mail, one a very boring circular and the fourth was addressed to Harri and not to me anyway! So I still don't know what has happened to all my letters.

DAY SEVENTYONE

My ribs seem to be getting more painful each day. However, not so painful that they prevented me from going to the camera shop to collect my new Nikon. It has a very sweet built-in motor drive and makes me feel just like Lord What's-his-name.

Sandra developed what looked like a sty a few weeks ago, but it never came to a head and has simply gone on growing. She finally took it to the doctor's this evening and he says that it is a cyst and has to come off. It is a local anaesthetic job I know, but still not very nice.

Dr Sherski confirmed that our decision to cancel Boss Hill was a wise one. "I think you should buy a small bungalow," he said. "You must be practical about this."

DAY SEVENTYTWO

I finally gave in and rang for an appointment about my ribs. I saw Dr Macaulay and she reckons the radiologist has cracked one. I now have to have an x-ray to find out what damage the previous x-ray did. This could go on indefinitely.

There was a stirring story on the news the other night about some people off the Greenpeace ship Sirius who tried to interfere with the West German incinerator ship Vesta from, as they claim, polluting the North Sea. They took off in a threatened force ten gale in inflatables to attempt a boarding of the German vessel. Travelling at speed and in quite heavy seas, they were hosed as they drew alongside. It all looked incredibly dangerous. A young girl however, did manage to get aboard and she chained herself to rails close to the incinerator. It was an astonishing performance.

Reading about it in the Times the following day, I discovered that the girl was Heather Holve. Heather was a wispy little kid who lived next door to us at Esher. Her father, ironically, is a chemical engineer and was partly responsible for awakening Jon's interest in geology.

Fifty or more years ago kids were likely to follow in father's footsteps; if dad was in insurance, son would usually go into insurance too. Today it is quite the reverse and whatever dad does is the last choice on earth for Sonny Jim. There is nought wrong with that I suppose, except that the decision often seems to be based on perversity rather than logic and that is not a good basis upon which to plan anything, least of all life, which is perversity personified!

DAY SEVENTYTHREE

I enjoy my food. My great passion is for classical French cooking and definitely not the nouvelle rubbish! I might have it all wrong I know, but I have experienced the nouvelle version, unfortunately, too many times in France to believe otherwise. It seems to offend a fundamental principle of haute cuisine when it assembles numerous different ingredients on the same plate. It is also over-preoccupied with the visual effects, sometimes at the expense of the flavour.

One of the many things I thought I would indulge myself with on retirement was learning to cook. I would love to have Floyd's casual skill and panache, but I would settle for considerably less. I have tried to cook over the years and my Welsh Rarebit is really quite good. But why is it that whatever I prepare tastes horrible at the table? Sandra can produce a delicious lunch from a few simple ingredients and yet when I try, using identical ingredients, it tastes awful? Perhaps cooks are born and not made.

I tried to produce a crab salad for lunch today. I love crab, but this version tasted horrible. The crab was all right, it was the choice of salad and the dressing I suppose which was wrong and this ruined the taste of the crab. I wish there were an afternoon class just around the corner I could go to. I bet there would be a big demand for such a facility. After I have learnt to cook I shall set one up.

Michael was a welcome visitor this afternoon, delivering the customary bottle of wine from their duty free allowance. He drove back 570 miles in one day - towing a caravan. I find that a mind-blowing feat. The most I ever did in one day was 425 miles. That felt pretty exhausting at the time and I was not towing a caravan either and was in a Porsche. I do not know how people do these things. Everyone else seems to be able to drive much faster than I can, completing a trip from A - B say, in half the time that it takes me and yet I was going like a bat out of hell.

I did drive from Hammersmith Broadway to the West Pier at Brighton once in 55 minutes. I insist that no one today could beat that! It was before the motorway was built and I was doing well over a hundred much of the way. It was 60 miles in 55 minutes, and a lot of it through built-up areas where speed had to be moderated.

There is little joy however, left in motoring today compared with the fifties and early sixties. Then there was just a comfortable amount of traffic on the open roads, allowing one to motor at one's own speed and not in convoy with three-deep traffic all travelling at ten miles per hour faster than the speed limit. My great delight was driving home at about 2 or 3 o'clock in the morning. I would pass about ten cars only between Maidstone and London. With the hood down and the heater on full blast, the headlights dancing in the mist, one could really enjoy the 'open road'. Never again I fear.

Today, whatever hour of the day or night, wherever you are, the roads teem with traffic. I gather that a net one and a half million additional cars come on to the roads in this country every year. One day the British Isles will sink under the weight of this iron and all these new motorcars will coagulate down in the centre of the earth and will become so dense that they will form a black hole! Heavens, the south east of England is already sinking.

DAY SEVENTYFOUR

Sandra came home early this afternoon to take me to the hospital for my ribs to be x-rayed. Just one picture, a full frontal. How the hell will they be able to check from that whether I have a cracked rib on my side?

And so it goes on.

We motored in to college after that to have another go at clearing my office out. Everyone thinks that this should be a traumatic experience for me. I do not mind it in fact. It is quite exciting unearthing relics I had long ago forgotten. I have a beautiful brass and mahogany plate camera made by Thornton Packard which I have not looked at for many years. I am not sure why it should have been at college in the first place. It has an amazingly Heath Robinson shutter mechanism, all string and springs, which still works giving shutter speeds from 1/30th to 1/90th of a second. It must have been one of the earliest shutters ever made.

Then there is the Japanese tin hat which I wore once to give a highly unpopular lecture. I don't know where that came from.

There were two plastic model aeroplanes, one of them a Spitfire, which I made when Jonathan was much younger. (And so was I!). I put them out on the grass at the side of the road in the hope that some appreciative boy might find them.

Old photographs of very young looking staff kept turning up. They made me feel very ancient.

The thing that does depress me in this exercise is the paper, mountains of dusty files which I have not got the courage to throw away and yet God knows why I want to keep them? I like to think that one day I will write a book about the Poly and all those crazy people who worked there. I could really get rid of all my prejudices and pet hates that I have been storing for the last thirty years. What a lot of enemies I could make of my friends, however.

There was one locked cupboard I had certain qualms about. Not having had the need to open it for years I now discovered I had lost the key. It contained my coin and stamp collections and the big question in my mind was were they still going to be there? Bryan Gauld, a structural engineer no less, succeeded in getting into the cupboard by unscrewing the side of it. The door then simply fell off. My collections were still there and I rediscovered how amazingly heavy coin collections are.

At the end of a dusty afternoon, during which many people popped their heads around the door to say hallo, there is still lots more to move. Perhaps one more trip will do it though and then I shall have to hand over the keys to the shop! I remember very clearly they were the words that Eric Brown used when he gave me the keys to his office on his compulsory retirement. Not a very happy recollection!

DAY SEVENTYFIVE
Another wet and cold Saturday. No Indian Summer this year.

British Telecom are getting a lot of stick lately about overcharging and general inefficiency. Just before the answering machine saga, we had two new phones fitted, a Freeway and a Venue. The Freeway is very useful as one can take it around the house and receive or make calls from wherever you are, like in the loo for example. The Venue is just a phone with lots of buttons and all sorts of facilities and memory stores.

British Telecom sent me a bill of £95 for the Venue, when it is on sale everywhere else at £75, including the BT shop in Bentalls! I queried this with them and they did send me an amended bill. But to make it even more irritating the darned thing stopped working a few days ago and we had to change it this morning at Wimbledon.

That was a hassle too. The girl tested it and of course it worked. I said that it was obviously an intermittent fault. She then suggested that it had been unplugged. I explained that one had to grovel on hands and knees behind a table, and that to unplug it was not an easy task.

She said, "But that would explain why it stopped working."

"I agree, but it was not unplugged in fact. No way could it have been unplugged without us knowing and it was not unplugged."

She shrugged her shoulders. " But it is working now."

"As I said before, it must have an intermittent fault."

She then started asking me how I had set the memory system up, convinced obviously of my imbecility.

"Look, I had a heart attack two months ago," I explained with heavy patience, "and I do not want to get angry with you. This telephone was properly installed and properly set up. It has worked for a number of weeks and then it stopped working. It was not unplugged and it now has an intermittent fault which you cannot detect. I do not propose to take it home and bring it back again to tell you that it is still not working."

She tossed her head, gathered the phone and said, "I haven't got a black one, will a white one do?" She could have said that right at the beginning and saved us both a lot of hassle.

I have now plugged the new white phone in - and guess what - it doesn't ring!

Fortunately the Freeway still bleeps for incoming calls, so we are not incommunicado. But can I face that beastly woman at Wimbledon again? It will probably ring when she tries it!

DAY SEVENTYSIX

The great adventure today is a trip down to Eastbourne, to have lunch with my brother-in-law Ron Blackstock, Michael's father.

My sister Vi died three years ago and Ron has made an amazing job of keeping his life together after that tragedy. He is 75, plays three rounds of golf a week and can out-walk his son, he is so fit.

He gave us a beautifully cooked and served roast beef lunch and afterwards we sat with our coffee admiring the splendid sea views which extend to include Beachy Head. There was a sea fret, but it lifted occasionally to show the tramp steamers slogging up the channel. There was a white pigeon and one lonely sea gull pecking busily away all afternoon on the grass in front of the veranda. Ron said they were both almost domesticated. He does feed them apparently. God, how I long to get out of London.

The drive down to Eastbourne was great and I had a definite lift as we turned on to the motorway and there was that splendid panorama to the southeast. I have not seen so much countryside for weeks and weeks.

The drive back was not so good. It had started raining before we left at dusk and by the time we got to Brighton it was dark and very wet. I hate motorways on wet, dark nights - and especially if someone else is driving. I am not casting aspersions on Sandra's driving here, because she is a very safe driver and that is more than one can say about half the motorists on the road. Twice, when joining one motorway from another, as we were adjusting our speed to slot in to an appropriate gap, we were overtaken on the inside by brainless press-on morons, one of whom was quite an elderly gentleman.

Which brings me to another one of my strongly held beliefs - that the driving test is pathetically inadequate. All it does is to test at a very rudimentary level that one can drive and control a car. It does not test that ability in night driving, or on motorways, or on wet and slippery roads. Nor does it test anything like road sense or sheer motoring ability as distinct from the mechanics of driving a car. Anyone can pass the test after ten or so hours dual instruction, then get straight into a high performance car and belt off up the motorway in sheeting rain. It is patently ridiculous, as most other European nations acknowledge where driving tests are considerably more stringent.

Logically drivers should be taught to drive under all the road conditions they will ever experience such as motorway driving, both day and night, night driving in the country as well as in town, and in rain and ice. How many drivers have actually practised skidding and indeed know how to control skids? Yet drivers who have never even experienced a skid will hare down the motorway in sheeting rain, putting every other driver in striking distance at mortal risk. What does the newly licensed driver know about aquaplaning? Very little, I suspect, when I am passed at speeds in excess of 80 on a streaming motorway.

I believe that the single most important quality a driver should develop is anticipation. To anticipate what the fool in front is about to do is the safest measure one can take on the road - short of staying at home. But anticipation comes only with much experience, just like the other aspects of road sense. Without road sense, or the craft of motoring, any driver is a bloody menace to other road users. So, newly licensed motorists, even much better taught and tested ones, are a hazard and should be so labelled. For twelve months after passing a test the driver should wear a 'novice' badge and only if he has twelve months of accident-free driving should he then qualify for a full licence.

I also believe that periodic re-testing should become the norm. As a flying instructor in the RAF I had periodic tests and it was possible to obtain a higher category if one demonstrated an improved performance. This was a positive incentive. To go from C category to B and then to A2 was a powerful ambition - no one actually ever made A1 to my knowledge! A lot of drivers already go in for the Advanced Motorist's Test which indicates that there is an interest in such a thing. If the re-test were compulsory it could incorporate the principles of the Advanced Motoring Test and if one could then sport a badge indicating superior ability, I believe it would go down very well. The objective is to improve driving skills and to develop road sense where the existing system does neither.

I am quite sure that many people will disagree with me, claiming that the present system is adequate and that common sense always prevails, ensuring that most drivers are adequate after the first few months. If so, then who are all these drivers then who persistently fling open their car doors in the face of approaching traffic? Who are all these drivers who, when turning right, position their cars so that following drivers cannot pass them on the nearside? Who are all these drivers who park on yellow lines just because they want to shop - and f... all the drivers who are trying to get past? Who are all these drivers who drive up on the pavement to park so that passing motorists are not inconvenienced - and f... the pedestrians! Road sense? A thing of the past! The present generation of motorists has never heard of it.

DAY SEVENTYSEVEN

Monday, the start of another week. I spent a lot of time this morning on the telephone, ringing Milan, Swansea, Lincoln and London. The Milanese call was to tell Alfa's when Jonathan expected to arrive, Swansea to ask when my driving licence is coming back, Lincoln for particulars of a house advertised in the Times and London to the RIBA.

Then I remembered that the cheap rate does not start until 1 o'clock!

DAY SEVENTYEIGHT

There was an incoming call recorded when I got back from shopping which, unfortunately, I did not see at that time.

It was Jonathan saying that he would be arriving in Milan an hour later than he had said. It was just about the original time he was due to arrive that I eventually got through to Signora Mobili at Alfa's. By then they had already sent a car to meet the original train and would not have another driver for the later train and general confusion all around. Why I should have been involved, here in London, escapes me.

It all worked out in the end apparently, as Jonathan explained when he rang later. They met him and got him to their hotel.

DAY SEVENTYNINE

Sandra came home at about 2.30, to take me to hospital for the results of my barium meal. I appear to have a hiatus hernia, which is no news at all. That, and the damage caused by the x-ray machine, seemed of little interest to Doctor Gunraj. He was hard put to think of what other tests I might have and what else he could do with me. I began to think he had run out of ideas when he came up with an 'Exercise ECG'. I tried to tell him that I could not do all this treadmill stuff even before the heart attack, but he thought it might be useful.

"We've given you all the other tests, we might as well do this one too."

He was uncertain about it to start with, saying something about letting my heart settle down first. I am sure I detected a hint of "If this doesn't kill you, you're cured."

Jonathan rang to say he was leaving Milan this evening and going back to France, to Plan de la Tour, just north of St. Tropez.

DAY EIGHTY

There was a superb house for sale in this week's Country Life. It had a flat roof - unfortunately - but otherwise it was just the sort of house I could well have designed for myself. The finishes are excellent, hardwood joinery inside and out and a splendidly equipped kitchen, Poggenpohl units, Neff cooking equipment and so on. It is gorgeously sited in an acre or so of gardens with super views of the sea. If it were in Sussex it would be on offer at about half a million pounds. It is however, in north Yorkshire, on the edge of the moors, beautiful country just north of Scarborough and for sale at a price we could afford. The thing is, do we live in the south, in a modest cottage and vegetable plot, or do we live in the north in a super house set in super surroundings?

I do not think that is any choice at all, but why does everybody we talk to about it immediately start shaking their heads, sucking in their breath through their teeth and generally putting on the doom? So it snows in Yorkshire. The trains stop running here in Surbiton at the first flurry of snow. Wet leaves are enough to close Waterloo Station! They might even have snowploughs in Yorkshire.

DAY EIGHTYONE

Michael drove us to the New Victoria Hospital this evening, for Sandra to have the cyst removed from her eyelid. She emerged after about fifteen minutes, her head dramatically covered in bandages. She declined the cup of tea they kindly offered her and we took her home to the more relevant hard stuff. I rate the medicinal value of whiskey very highly and it is the one vice I have yet to be denied - Thank God.

DAY EIGHTYTWO

When Sandra removed the bandage from her eye last night we were surprised at not seeing a wound. The surgeon had obviously rolled her eyelid up and had made the necessary cut to remove the cyst on the inside of the lid. We were also surprised that her eye lid looked much the same as it did before she had the cyst removed, that is, very inflamed and swollen and painful and much more so!

We are having some people in for dinner this evening, which seems a daft idea to me, but Sandra thought it would take her mind off her eye. I suppose that is some sort of logic.

It was a busy day too, quite a lot to distract Sandra, if that is what's required. We finally moved the computer into the study and liberated the dining room in the process. That simple move involved a switch around which in turn involved the entire house; hardly a piece of furniture remained in its original starting place.

It all took too long of course, leaving little enough time to do the shopping. We got back home, tired, irritable and edging towards panic. Entertaining should be a pleasure.

Well, in the event it is, of course, it's just the preparation which is such a bind. I can imagine some people saying that's rubbish too, but I'm not a masochist.

Fortunately our guests were all late arriving and we were just about ready for them with the champers properly chilled.

Sandra did a super dinner, Dublin Bay prawns and oysters shipped from France only yesterday with a dry white

134

Burgundy, followed by fillet steak and peppered chef's butter with a rich red Cabernet Sauvignon and then a crème caramel for pudding.

The only disappointment for me was the poor reception the idea got of living in Yorkshire. Everyone made so much of the climate and of the fact that we would be snowed up every winter. It is astonishing how Londoners view the north of England as though it were another country. Sandra has a curious reaction too, as a Lancastrian by birth she feels obliged to have reservations, although not seriously I guess.

DAY EIGHTYTHREE

I probably overdid things yesterday because I had a bad night with palpitations and a rattling pulse rate. I sat in front of the tele and dozed most of the day. I do recall seeing something of that excellent film "The Battle of Britain" with lots of footage of the real thing in it. Amazingly it doesn't date as so much of the contemporary cinema does.

I also saw Nigel Mansell fail in the Portuguese Grand Prix, or rather his car fail. I did not watch the first match of the football season!

DAY EIGHTYFOUR

I still feel a bit shagged. It is quite salutary really how much Saturday seems to have taken out of me. The margins are quite narrow it appears - I must keep on taking the tablets!

I got myself a salad lunch and then felt very wicked when I turned the tele on while eating. It was a western, Billy the Kid and Doc Holliday. I was just going to turn it off when I recognised the large boobs Billy was wrestling with in the hay - they could only belong to Jane Russell and I remembered how they turned me on the first time I saw "The Outlaw". It was disappointing to find that they did little for me now. However, because of her mammaries, or the acting, which I doubt, I sat and watched the whole thing through.

DAY EIGHTYFIVE
Feeling marginally stronger I walked up to the surgery to collect a letter for my car insurance company. The doctor says I can drive once more, but the insurance people are being very cautious and want it in writing. Having the car again will transform everything. I will no longer be a prisoner bounded by the distance my two feet will take me.

Peter called on his way home from college and I showed him the house in Yorkshire. He was extremely enthusiastic about it, quite the reverse of the Saturday people. He will buy it he says, if I don't. That was much more what I wanted to hear.

I was also delighted to learn that he has been short-listed for the headship at Canterbury. I think he should get that one, I so hope so, although it will leave Kingston in a spot. They are unlikely now to get a new head in post before next academic year, time enough for things to fall horribly apart. Without adequate leadership and with such a strong staff, each of whom is a virtuoso, things will go off in umpteen different directions at once.

DAY EIGHTYSIX
It is Sandra's birthday tomorrow and New Malden is not exactly the West End for shopping. I walked the High Street

for inspiration. It was good exercise, but thin on birthday pressies.

The ritual is for me to cook the dinner on Sandra's birthday, but when you stop to think about it, that's a daft ritual. What sort of treat is it to have me cook the dinner? I spent half the day reading cookbooks - not so much for inspiration, more out of desperation really. I settled on Spicy Scallops, a delicious dish of scallops in dry sherry, soy sauce, ginger and chopped spring onion, amongst others. The fish shop had no scallops! I had to do a quick adjustment to accommodate what they had got. Prawns!

Prawn Pilaf, brown rice and peppers. Not really in the same league, but it will have to do, perhaps topped with fresh strawberries and cream?

Jon rang from Elba! He was in Plan de la Tour, on the Cote d'Azur, just a few days ago.

DAY EIGHTYSEVEN
It was a busy day, wrapping Sandra's 'toe cover' and getting ready for dinner. The blasted prawns took at least an hour to de-armour.

I guess dinner was alright. Sandra said it was, without being too condescending about it. I would really like to be able to cook though. I'll take her out to dinner next year! Next year?

DAY EIGHTYEIGHT
We had thought of going up to Yorkshire this coming weekend, but the weather is not too promising, so we cancelled out. Norfolk seemed more manageable and we dug

out the numerous houses we had received recently and started telephoning estate agents. Not one of them was unsold however. We should have gone to Scarborough!

DAY EIGHTYNINE

Failing Yorkshire and Norfolk - we drove down to Dorking.

The place is full of antique shops; £4,500 for a simple mahogany side-table seemed to be the norm. It provokes me to filthy profanity. Someone somewhere has got their values screwed up.

There can be no justification in such absurd excesses. There must be an enormous surplus of money floating around to encourage dealers to such outrageous levels. £4,500, or half to a third of the average low-level annual income, on a side table? .... It is morally indefensible. And incredibly, many old age pensioners still wobbly pop their 'Maggie Thatcher' vote into the ballot box!

DAY NINETY

There were splashes of blood on the staircase this morning. Then we saw more blood in the cat's dish. We found Felix, a miserably hunched bunch of fur, with blood oozing from his ear. He does take his role as Estate Senior Cat very seriously and is constantly fighting to keep down the lesser cats. One in particular, a lovely white moggy called Bella, is a very confused cat. She is, after all, a he and having been given a name like that it is no wonder she, I mean he, fights. Even cats can have hang-ups!

Jon rang from Paris. He is coming home on Tuesday.

DAY NINETYONE

A real landmark, my driving licence has been reinstated. I have not driven for three months, but at last I am liberated. It was quite a thrill to get the car out of the garage and to drive into Kingston. I went to the Town Planning Department at the Guildhall to look at the planning proposal for the site adjoining Fairacre. It is for thirty-four sheltered units, or flats for the disabled.

I have no objection in principle to such a development, but when I see that it is to take the form of four-storey high blocks, without lifts, and that one of the blocks is to be three feet away from the rear of my patio, I had to warn the planning assistant that they will be hearing further from me.

How can the planners take such a proposal seriously? Imagine the elderly and disabled climbing up four storeys to get home. The point is of course, that the developers can cram more such units onto the site than they could normal flats. They will be laughing all the way to the bank!

It is a pretty shabby business, this speculative development racket. The developers for this scheme probably know that it will not be approved, but they work to the principle that if you put in some outrageous proposal it can always be cut back until you reach the maximum the planners will allow. The hazard here for the rest of us with this ploy is that they can get away with more than they should by wearing the planners down.

How nice it would be if these developers could first take regard of the environment and establish what might best benefit it, rather than their pockets all the time. While the planners have considerable authority in such matters they can only reject schemes - they cannot tell the developer what he should build.

The other party involved in such enterprises is, of course, the architect and he is the one who is condemned for any outrageous development, rather than the developer. In a sense this is justifiable as he is very well qualified to know what is and what is not suitable in any situation. As a student I used to say I will refuse such commissions, but the reality I found was that there was always another architect down the road, with a mortgage and five hungry children, who would not refuse. And why should he? I have never heard of a lawyer refusing to take on the defence of a criminal, so why should the architect be the only one restrained by morality and be expected to act as an unpaid environment watchdog? Prince Charles, please note.

Having said all that, I really cannot condone the architect who designs four storey blocks without lifts for the disabled within three feet of single storey patios!

DAY NINETYTWO

Jon arrived home after lunch from Paris, having done 10,000 miles on a £100 train pass. His best comment to date is - "If St Tropez was ankle deep in cigarette butts, Marbella was knee deep in condoms."

Felix, who has been visiting the vet daily since his fight, was signed off this evening. He is the world's worst car traveller and it takes both of us to get him anywhere, one to drive and the other to smother the cat. The problem of how we will transport Felix to another part of the country when we move bothers me.

We took him down to Brighton once where I had a cottage. It was a nightmare. He did everything imaginable - and unimaginable - mostly over Sandra. I had to stop to let

Jonathan out as he was threatening to be sick as well. Not like Fingal, our first cat, (so named because we had her when we lived in a cavelike basement flat at Surbiton) who would curl up to sleep blissfully in the car until we had arrived somewhere. She was amazing actually, she would sleep until we turned into our road at Brighton and then she would sit up, but always at the same corner.

The cottage at Brighton was terraced and it had a wee walled garden at the back. Fingal disappeared one afternoon having last been seen sitting on the wall. We searched the house and the neighbourhood, but no Fingal. That evening I went into the basement room in the front of the house and there in the basement area outside the window was Fingal sitting on the window cill.

Just how that cat got out of the garden and into the street is a mystery to start with. All the back gardens were entirely enclosed and she could only have got into the street by going through a neighbour's house. From enquiries while we were looking for her it was clear that she could not have been through a house in Queen's Gardens, but must have penetrated one in the next road behind Queen's Gardens. From there she must have wandered down to North End Road, which has a lot of traffic pounding up and down, round the corner into Queen's Gardens, up to the cottage and then squeezed herself down past a wire net grill into the basement area. How the hell she knew it was the right cottage is baffling because she had only ever been carried from the car into the house - and this only three times in her life.

Fingal was a very intelligent cat, not like some cats I could mention!

DAY NINETYTHREE

Leaving Jon sleeping off his exhaustion, I drove up to Kensington High Street to shop for an enlarger bulb. It is great to be mobile again. It would appear that my type of enlarger bulb is no longer made, or was that the stock answer one usually gets when the shopkeeper is out of stock? Why do they play that stupid game? Presumably they hope to sell you an alternative, but my reaction is to find another shop.

DAY NINETYFOUR

Another hectic day of shopping - cat food, Flora and fruit juice. Anything to keep the cholesterol level down.

If anything is calculated to raise my blood pressure it must be a meeting of the Estate management committee. I am all for keeping the maintenance charge as low as possible, but this evening's meeting was silly. Betty was very Bolshie. With a predicted surplus of only £80 for the year and nothing put aside for contingencies, she insisted that the maintenance charge be the same as for last year. Evelyn, a colleague from the Polytechnic, was more concerned about my blood pressure than the maintenance charge.

As we are going up to Scarborough tomorrow for a long weekend, I would have preferred a quieter evening.

DAY NINETYFIVE

A beautiful sunny day and Scarborough in daylight looked delightful. From the cliff-side one has a splendid view of the bay and the ravine-like road slicing inland to the town with its attractive wrought iron bridge high overhead.

I am quite sold on Scarborough. It reminds me a little of Brighton - not to everyone's taste - with its Victorian architecture and wrought iron and its defiant air of respectability. I feared to find it full of trashy seaside clichés, the candyfloss and the slot machines. It does have lots of these of course, but in muted moderation so that they do not shout at you. Scarborough has not one, but three harbours; one for working fishing boats, another for pleasure boats and a third for small pleasure craft.

In contrast with the town, the house we had motored all this way to see was a disappointment. It was ideally located on the cliffs at Cloughton, a village just north of Scarborough, with superb sea views and cliff-side walks. The countryside is lovely and I would be very happy to live here. But the house was not as described - two of the five bedrooms were windowless cupboards and an entire elevation of glass and timber framing needed rebuilding.

If an estate agent got himself a reputation for writing honest blurbs about the houses he was selling he would make a killing.

However, estate agents are either not very intelligent, or they think we aren't. I am becoming an authority on the breed.

DAY NINETYSEVEN
The sun disappeared and it rained for the drive home. We splashed off at 11.30 am, but in spite of the dreary weather it was not too bad a trip with only one detour near Sheffield where the M18 was closed. We did 575 miles, sharing the driving.

The best recollection of the trip was the breakfast we had this morning - eggs, bacon, tomatoes, mushrooms, fried bread, coffee, toast and marmalade - and I'm supposed to be losing weight! What frustrates me is that Sandra can put such food away without adding an inch to her waist. Just reading the menu puts inches on mine!

DAY NINETYEIGHT

Jon starts the MSc in Structural Geology today at Imperial College - without any grant assistance whatever. I am staking him, with the help of a small insurance policy Sandra took out to benefit him after he graduated. I guess it is going to do just that, but not in the way we anticipated.

The grant system is neither predictable nor adequate. While a mandatory grant is available to everyone for a first degree, a grant for a second, or Master's, is discretionary. That is to say that the local authority concerned can say yes or no to any application. On the face of it that may seem not unreasonable, the snag is that some authorities are far more generous than others and it so happens that Kingston must be the meanest authority in the country! If you are lucky enough to have a West Country address you might well get a grant for a second degree, but not if you live in the Royal Borough. Kingston is further right than Maggie herself. So, what do they spend their money on? Some would say car stackers these days - anything to get the people in to boost the local commerce.

There are some bursaries available which are usually awarded on merit. There were two this year on Jon's MSc course, but they did not go very far amongst fifteen candidates. I question the criterion of merit anyway, rather than need. I have seen too many candidates who were fortunate enough to get one of these scarce bursaries 'piss it up the wall' as they say, while their lesser colleagues struggle on manfully in spite of the crippling hardship of having no money. It is much easier to assess financial hardship than it is to assess potential for a course of study.

DAY NINETYNINE
I rang the estate agent in Yorkshire and offered £100,000 for the house in Scarborough. He rang back a bit later and said it was not enough. So, bye, bye, Yorkshire - you are too greedy.

I went up to the RIBA this afternoon (and if you want to upset an architect call it Reeba!) to chair the Appeals Committee, one of my few remaining professional responsibilities. I do not know how long this committee has existed but I have been attending its meetings for the last twenty-five years at least. Over this time I have met many agreeable colleagues on it like Kenneth Campbell, the ex-housing architect for the GLC, Edward D Mills whose work I admired as long ago as my student days, John Moon who occupied the chair at the Bartlett with much distinction and David Farrant who seems to have persisted for as long as I. But then one did meet the same people over the years on committee after committee.

The role of this committee is to hear the appeals from candidates who have failed the external examinations four times, the maximum number of sittings allowed by the rules. It is heart-breaking sometimes to hear the sad tales of misguided endeavour from elderly men who, having spent their working lives trying to qualify, now find themselves forever debarred by the regulations. However, I have only known of one candidate ever being denied a fifth opportunity and the work of the committee is really in giving advice to the candidate, probably the first they have had in their lives, to ensure that the fifth time will be successful.

Alan Palmer, the RIBA Examinations Officer, has always organized the work of this committee and I found him this afternoon as calm, gentle and efficient as he was twenty-five years ago when I first met him.

The candidates were as ever, misinformed, misguided and generally sad cases. If only they would seek advice much earlier in their careers, they would save themselves so much wasted time and effort. One of them, a man of fifty-three, blamed his wife for his failure. He said she gave him no help, nagged him and crowded out his study time. His appeal was based upon the fact that he was getting a divorce and that from hereon he would be able to study. We spent forty minutes trying to persuade him that until he admitted that it was he who had failed and not his wife he would never make good his deficiency.

With the phasing out of the external examinations - that is, examinations taken at the RIBA rather than at a recognised school of architecture - one hopes that these sad people will disappear from the system.

DAY ONE HUNDRED

This should be a significant day, the one hundredth after my heart attack. So, what momentous things have happened to mark the occasion? Not a lot! I never even noticed that it was a significant day.

I wrote the planning objection to the development on the adjoining site to Fairacre and I doubt whether the developer noticed anything unusual either.

DAY ONE HUNDRED AND ONE

Now this day was a bit more significant - the day I had to go to hospital to have an exercise ECG. It was a bad time.

Fully wired up, I was then put on a treadmill and told that I had to keep going and on no account to chicken out. It was fine to start with, like walking up the road, but then the treadmill started going faster - and not only faster but uphill as well. A devilish bit of equipment. In the end I was running uphill, a thing I have avoided for years.

After a quarter of an hour I had to call it off - before I fell off. The room was spinning like a top and I had a galaxy of stars in my vision. They helped me back to a chair and left me to recover - or perhaps to die! I thought about it and decided to recover.

There followed an odd conversation between the doctor and the nurse about elementary maths. The doctor was not very good at sums and concluded that I was dead as he studied the printout. The nurse could plainly see that I was not dead and corrected his arithmetic to prove it. Thank God she was there because the doctor didn't have a clue.

He then summarised the results by saying that my heart was performing normally and that the cause of my breathlessness was probably the medication. If I were his patient he said he would take me off the propranolol.

He did say that my blood pressure was abnormally low and that alone would account for my shortness of breath.

"So, why is my blood pressure low?" I asked.

"That's a very good question," he said. He never did give me an answer.

England beat the West Indies in the World Cup in India today. Amazing!

DAY ONE HUNDRED AND TWO

I felt shagged out, breathless and tired and dozed in the armchair all day. Blasted ECG!

DAY ONE HUNDRED AND THREE

The weather is both cold and wet. I feel both cold and wet - well, rung out anyway.

We drove to Tesco to do the weekend shopping and I had my usual hate campaign about the otherwise healthy, but selfish, bastards who park in the bays reserved for the disabled.

It seems to be a symptom of our uncaring society which makes me more angry than is good for me. It is not done in error either, because when challenged the offenders show guilt, or become abusive - but never surprise. I saw one robust looking man limp painfully from his car to the store and then walk briskly through the entrance. Another young lad in green wellies and a Barbour jacket told me once that I had no breeding when I asked him what his disability was. As he was about to shop in MFI I wondered if that, or the green wellies, constituted breeding.

Of the twelve reserved spaces for the disabled at Tesco only one today was legitimately occupied. God knows how that one managed to fight off all those fit and healthy 'cripples'.

The subtlety with the disabled parking bays of course, is not just that they are close to the entrance, but that they have extra width to enable the disabled more easily to struggle out of their cars with the doors wide open. So, these healthy, but moronic, self-immersed, sub-humans squeeze their cars into these inviting gaps thus not only depriving some poor lame sod a convenient parking space, but destroying the whole concept designed to make life just a wee bit easier for the afflicted. How selfish can you get?

The factor that astonishes me is that it is not a transgression restricted to just a few of the car-driving public, but that it is commonplace. Have we, all of us, really lost our sense of compassion for the less fortunate? Maggie's society is a devastatingly 'hang-you-Jack-I'm-fireproof' society, but surely we have not yet reached the level of kicking the cripple's crutches from underneath him - or have we?

DAY ONE HUNDRED AND FOUR

I suppose one must expect the weather to be unpleasant in October, but one does not have to stay here to enjoy it. If we all emigrated just think what it would do to the house prices and all those estate agents who would have to go off to find an honest living. The disabled wouldn't have any trouble parking either.

DAY ONE HUNDRED AND FIVE

I have not yet got over that exercise ECG and I still feel a bit grim and short of breath. I put the TV on to watch the cricket but it had been washed out - in Pakistan for heaven's sake! How far does this depression extend?

So, I had a snooze and then drove to Ealing to call on my accountant about the capital gains tax. It was pissing with rain and because of that, or because I did not want to talk to any one about capital gains anyway, I could not find his office.

DAY ONE HUNDRED AND SIX

Peter collected me at 9.30 this morning to take me out to an antique dealer friend of his to look at antique clocks. My retirement fund he told me stands at £1,900! It is unbelievable.

There is no way I can think of to thank everyone other than perhaps through this diary even though no one will ever see it!

Contributions came from all over, the Middle East, Africa and so on. One ex-student was flying back from Africa for the evening of the original party. It makes me feel that those thirty years were not such a waste of time after all.

I chose a beautiful Viennese, ebony-lined, walnut striking Regulator of about 1860. It was like all one's birthdays come true to be given the choice of half-a-dozen magnificent clocks like that. (And there I was not long ago saying how obscene it was to pay £4,500 for a side table - which didn't even chime!)

Peter brought me home and we had a good lunch which Sandra had left for us - smoked salmon with the 'fruit of the sturgeon' and a well-chilled Sauvignon.

Unable to think of anything which could cap the morning's excitement I typed the minutes of the last Management Committee meeting instead and a letter to my neighbours asking for their maintenance money. I have never been a company director before and it is entirely consistent that this one is unpaid, unwanted and unlikely!

DAY ONE HUNDRED AND SEVEN

Everyone was at home this afternoon so we all went shopping at Marks and Sparks. It was a bad day for Sandra who paid and Jonathan and I came home with new woollies and sweaters. I left them at their peak of shopping fever and went back to the car as I felt giddy.

'You must live a normal life and forget all about the heart attack' the medics say, but when one is constantly reminded by some abnormality like this it is very difficult to comply. Although one is not morbidly preoccupied with it one does have a sense of vulnerability lurking in the back of one's mind all the time.

I do not think that anything like enough attention is given to the psychological effects of a heart attack. The patient is warned about it but is not advised on how to deal with it. I thought that the psychological effects would wear off with time and regained confidence. But this does not seem to be so. If anything, the sense of mortality increases.

The fact that there is still only a teenager inside this decrepit old body only adds to the confusion of course.

DAY ONE HUNDRED AND EIGHT

I finally found the accountant today in Ealing and briefed him about my capital gains tax assessment. He sounded confident enough - confident that he will save me his fees, but I feel that is not quite the point!

There was a phone call from Harri Ap Rees when I got back inviting me to introduce the principal guest at the Faculty Degree Ceremony at the Guildhall next February. It pleased me no end and I think it a very thoughtful gesture on the part of the Faculty. I shall see all those students who graduated and diplomated last July and who I deserted so abruptly a few weeks earlier.

The barometer is falling dramatically. It registered 955 on my wall 'met office' when I went to bed and sure enough the wind awakened me at 3.30 am. It sounded really boisterous and I got up and checked all the windows for security. The lean-to greenhouse against the living room windows seemed the most vulnerable and I feared it would be blown away pane by pane.

151

I suppose we slept thereafter on and off, but it was a very disturbing night. I have never heard wind like it before. The severity of the storm was then dramatised even more by a power cut at 6.30 am. We gave up trying to sleep at that point and got up and put a battery driven radio on.

The news was brief at first, but it began to expand as it trickled in. It really had been an horrendous night in the southeast and everywhere was in chaos. Transport was halted by fallen trees, no trains or buses were running and people were advised not to attempt any journey whatsoever. Hurricane force winds reached gusts of 110 mph in London and it was confirmed that the barometric pressure went as low as 956 millibars. Sandra obviously could not get over to Highgate although at one stage she was determined to try; she wanted to take the car.

DAY ONE HUNDRED AND TEN

A tremendous amount of damage was caused by the storm and just locally, in Acacia Grove, trees were blown down and the street littered with roof slates and tiles. Some houses had very ugly gaps in their roofs. At Fairacre the damage was limited to three silver birches which lost their tops but which fortunately blew away from the parked cars. Had I known that we were in the middle of a hurricane the night before last I would have been terrified.

DAY ONE HUNDRED AND ELEVEN

There is nothing like a hurricane to arouse the community spirit. Half the estate turned out this morning, Sunday, to tidy up the trees and to clear up the mess generally.

My first wife, Joan, returns from Italy this afternoon and a neighbour of hers rang me to ask if there was anyway I could get word to her before she gets home. She has three or four acres of beautiful gardens including a couple of lakes surrounded by immense elms and chestnuts. She had three or four acres of beautiful gardens that is, now all the trees are down and there is general devastation. Fortunately, I was able to warn her, otherwise she would have had a terrible shock.

DAY ONE HUNDRED AND TWELVE

Tomorrow I am to attend my belated retirement party, put off from last July. I have been making notes for months for the mandatory speech and today I got down to typing something. I am not looking forward to it. I fear that I shall not be able to handle it and that I will not perform as everyone would have me perform.

I am warned that there will over a hundred people there and many of them ex-students from decades ago. It will be doubly charged too because I shall be meeting colleagues whom I have not seen since my heart attack.

DAY ONE HUNDRED AND THIRTEEN

I was very pleased that Jonathan said he wanted to come to the retirement party. He and Sandra arrived home together at 5 o'clock and tossed up as to who should have the bathroom first. I was ready before they got back, determined that I would take the whole event as slowly as possible.

All I have been told of the arrangements is that my nephew Michael is taking us so that we do not have to worry about drinking and driving. A bit hard on Michael! He arrived on schedule at 7 o'clock saying that he had the strictest instructions to get me there by 7.30. I am beginning to feel quite festive.

We drove into the staff car park at Knights Park and there was my normal reserved bay, only this time highly decorated and framed with balloons and a large notice - Reserved for Him. This was Steve's work, the school's technician, I gathered.

My heart was thumping as we walked round the quadrangle. Everywhere was so strangely deserted - it was like the beginning of a Hitchcock thriller. Michael took us up to the Senior Common Room and opened the door and there it was - my retirement party - a great sea of faces beaming at me. Waiting to greet me just inside the door was Bob Smith the Director with his wife Rose, Phil Wookey Deputy Director, Charles Potts Acting Dean, Reg Bailey Chairman of Governors, Daphne Brooker Head of Fashion and Peter and Lesley Jacob. The partition between the SCR and the Refectory had been removed, tables of food inserted and beyond the food were hundreds of familiar faces - faces from now and faces from fifteen, twenty and even thirty years ago! It was an amazingly vivid moment.

Peter had planned things with great thought and thoroughness. He had briefed everyone apparently, before I had arrived, that I was not to be overwhelmed and that only two or three people should talk to me at a time. Everyone observed this injunction and though I damn the reason for it I guess it did make things easier for me.

It was a truly memorable evening meeting ex-students whom I had not seen for so many years and each of whom recalled some cameo of a memory long since overlooked. There was even an ex-member of staff, a colleague from the fifties. People had travelled from all over the country and it was very gratifying to find that all the ex-students there, with only one single exception, were partners in their own practices. That was an amazing statistic and I doubt that any other school could match it.

The conversations could fill many pages, but they were mostly of personal recollections which, while dear to me, would bore others.

So, we came to the speeches. Peter had done his research very well, recalling things I couldn't even remember. He was also very funny. Both he and Bob however, gave the impression that I was a crusty old so-and-so, particularly with people who used my parking bay. On reflection, maybe they had a point. Sandra said so too!

I was not supposed to know about the Viennese Regulator, but my delight was nevertheless quite spontaneous when I unveiled it at Reg Bailey's invitation, to say nothing of my reaction to the dozen bottles of my favourite whiskey and the twenty-four Edinburgh Lead Crystal glasses which surrounded it.

It was a good party. We left at about 11 o'clock, that is before a member of staff from the Law school took exception to a caretaker closing the piano lid on his fingers.

I am now conscious that I really have retired and that tomorrow I start the rest of my life.

POSTSCRIPT

Having survived the first 112 days after his heart attack, Dennis settled into retirement by writing several books covering his life, his research topics of *Creativity* and *Modern Architecture*, and an unfinished sci-fi novel called *The Thing* based on an architectural practice.

He carried on his academic pursuits for a further five years, teaching *Creativity* and *Modern Architecture* to students of the University of Notre Dame at their London Centre. History repeated itself with a second heart attack in 1992, however, so he concentrated for a while on his other loves of cars, cats and cricket.

Plans to move out of London were shelved, and Dennis radically redesigned the house at Fairacre. In 2000 he was diagnosed with kidney failure, but still went on to become the first Chair of The Groves Medical Centre Patients Group and, in 2004, the first Chair of Kingston Hospital Patients Forum. Prints of several of his paintings can now be found on the walls of Kingston Hospital.

Dennis died in August 2005, eighteen years after *That Heart Attack*.

DENNIS BERRY

The same day, the year after

BOOKS BY NUMBER 11 PUBLISHING

WHAT DID YOU DO IN THE WAR, DADDY? How did you help us to win?

By Dennis Berry, published September 2007
The first part of his autobiography, from 1939-1946
ISBN 978-0-9555134-1-1
210 x 148 mm, 196 pp with b&w and colour illustrations

THAT HEART ATTACK
and the next 112 days

By Dennis Berry, published November 2008
The defining moment when his life changed forever
ISBN 978-0-9555134-4-2
210 x 148 mm, 171 pp with b&w and colour illustrations

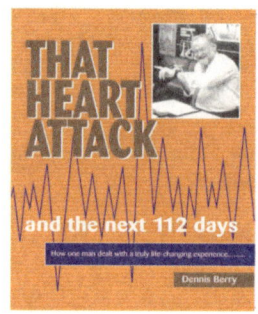

SAGA 2

By Dennis Berry, to be published in 2009
The second part of his autobiography, from 1946 to 2005

TIME FOR CHANGE
The Genesis of Modern Architecture

By Dennis Berry, to be published in 2009

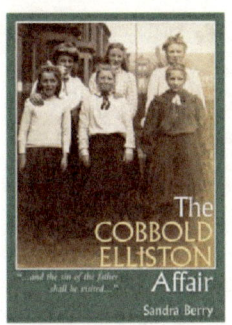

THE COBBOLD ELLISTON AFFAIR
'... and the sin of the father shall be visited ...'
By Sandra Berry, published February 2007
ISBN 978-0-9555134-0-4
210 x 148 mm, 184 pp with b&w illustrations

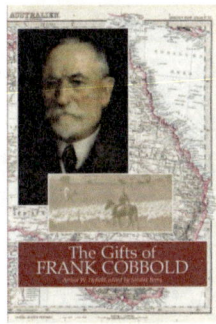

THE GIFTS OF FRANK COBBOLD
Originally written by Arthur W Upfield (1935), edited by Sandra Berry for *The Cobbold Family History Trust*, published October 2008
ISBN 978-0-9555134-3-5
234 x 156 mm, 280 pp with b&w & colour illustrations

KINGSTON PATIENTS FORUMS – The Legacy of their Work from January 2004 to March 2008
Edited by Sandra Berry, published March 2008
ISBN 978-0-9555134-2-8
297 x 210 mm, 104 pp with colour illustrations

163